HOW TO MAKE IT FROM A NO-TO-WHOA BUDGET

A New Filmmaker's Pocketbook Guide

Tazito Garcia

ACKNOWLEDGMENTS

I'd love to thank the following people for all their help, input, opinions and support throughout the process of creating this book: Paul Chang, Rorie McIntosh, Stephanie Herrera, Jessie Raymond and Maryam Mamipour. I would also like to extend a very special thank you to Zinaida Sze-To for staying up late for a whole week and helping with rearranging my ideas together.

Contents

ABOUT THE AUTHOR

Tazito Garcia is a multi-award winning writer, filmmaker and charismatic actor. His dominance in the independent filmmaking scene begun in the early 2000s. Specializing in crafting action-packed, thrilling stories with groundbreaking roles, Taz pushes boundaries and hones his creativity. His ambitious *grabbing life by the horns* approach and straightforward, *just do it* attitude launched his career and continues to drive him forward in the entertainment industry. Garcia is a university graduate with a major in *Hospitality and Tourism Management,* and a minor in Sales/ Marketing and Psychology. He incorporates all such facets of his education and expertise to convert his ideas to reality, embellish his work and enhance its marketability.

Tazito is an active member of the film community, having over two decades of hands-on experience, ranging from working in the Mecca of film—*Hollywood,* to the east, such as Malaysia and China. When he's not near a camera, he is often travelling the world for inspiration, conjuring innovative ideas and writing new content. Giving back and gratitude has always been vital to Taz, hence his passion for working with charities and philanthropic organizations of any size.

As a guest speaker at multiple film school ceremonies, he loves to inspire youth and support creative minds. Taz is keen to connect people, being a host of several industry events, and as an athlete, it is his passion to constantly push his mind and body for any acting role. Upon the creation of a string of no-budget-films, Garcia has motivated and encouraged many around the globe to pursue their dreams in spite of their obstacles.

"PICK UP A CAMERA, SHOOT SOMETHING,

NO MATTER HOW SMALL, NO MATTER HOW CHEESY, NOW YOU ARE A DIRECTOR."

— JAMES CAMERON

DISCLAIMER

Please don't do anything silly, kill yourself or put others at risk when creating art. This book presents a wide range of opinions and personal experiences related to film, filmmaking, operations, legalities and individuals. Create responsibly and treat everyone the same way you would want to be treated.

HOW TO USE THIS BOOK

You can read through this book chronologically or you can jump between each chapter if you are a compulsive note-taker. Remember, this pocket guide will help you think big for very little and make that film from A-Z when everyone says "how can that be?"

> **"It always seems impossible until it's done"**

- Nelson Mandela

TAO OF THE NO-BUDGET-FILMMAKER

Filmmaking is one of the most distinctive art forms. Not only is it a leading source of entertainment stirring an array of emotions, it is an extraordinarily powerful platform for educating, documenting, showcasing the profoundness of human culture, creativity and societal norms or lack there-of.

Filmmaking is a journey that is about self-discovery. It is all about making mistakes and learning from them. Filmmaking is a story behind the story.

As an early filmmaker, you will realize how you will need to understand every filmmaking position, how each and every role is essential to create an amazing final picture, and how at times, you just might need to fill a position or two when creating your own no-to-low budget films. The goal is to learn to communicate your visions clearly with people and not be shy to ask for what you need. Bear in mind to always provide value before you ask for something or favor. Whether you deem yourself an introvert or extrovert, continued communication is the key, and the communication will only get better with time. Remember, practice makes perfect.

Feeling inspired and ready to learn about filmmaking on a no-to-low budget? I hope you are ready because this book will open your eyes to the fundamentals of filmmaking and guide you through your journey from script to screen.

Get ready. Good luck and make sure you invite me to your screening!

Taz A. Garcia

DEDICATION

First, I would like to dedicate this book to my mother and grandmother, who have taught me that there are no limits except those we put within ourselves.

Second, I am not a self-made man and I have been fortunate enough to get a lot of help from supportive friends, family and complete strangers. They took a chance on an insanely creative individual with a vision. Thank you to each and every one of you who has made all my films possible. I am forever grateful!

"The only safe thing in filmmaking is to take a chance."

— Mike Nichols

FRAME YOUR MIND

What kind of content creator am I?

Everyone is capable of creating content these days. As many would phrase it "pumping out" content on various social media platforms has become the norm. The technology and ease of access has increased the competition in creating short clips or skits with an immediate measure of success or failure. As a result, content has flooded the platforms and audiences are overwhelmed by information. In turn, the attention span of viewers is significantly reduced over time. Nevertheless, this is the best time to take advantage of this era as the training grounds for you to hone your craft. It is the perfectly cheap and convenient method to introduce your body of work to audiences and potential producers around the globe.

With this in mind, we need to first figure out what type of content creator you are and what your directing style is. Content is all around us every day. We repeatedly discuss what we enjoy and prefer, along with what we dislike and the aspects we would change. This is often where our visions spark and our desire for creation is ignited. But, before we get to creating, we need to find your style. What drives you and why is this important?

Let's take a minute to decide what type of content you want to be creating. What **genre** of film would you want your film to be?

Is it an action blockbuster, a cult classic, a comedy or a silent film?

Once you have answered those questions, you move on to decide what type of director you are. From my experience as a filmmaker, giving directions and taking directions—as an actor—I have categorized four prominent types of directors. Take a look at which one you identify with most.

WHAT IS YOUR TYPE?

1. **The Actor's Director:** Many of these types of directors have a history of acting or theater. They favor performance heavy characters and often lean towards character driven scripts. They love to work with actors and actors love to work with them because they can connect on their level.

2. **The Writer Director:** These types like to write and direct. They are very connected to the written work and possess a strong desire in sticking to the script. They tend to be the least flexible of directors in terms of changes to the dialogue. Occasionally, they are willing to trade a line for a better performance. Their drive often stems from the passionate wish to adhere to the original idea.

3. **The Visionary Director:** Tends to be more technical and visual. Their focus tends to be on cinematography, production design or visual effects. Many of such directors come from a technical background, with the desire to transition and apply such skills into their projects.

4. **The Poetic Director:** This type of directing approach concentrates on the artistic aspects. They tend to exercise philosophical ideologies, visual symbolism and musical expression when storytelling. They break the norms, push boundaries and love to experiment new methods of storytelling. You can expect to watch content from the Poetic Director multiple times to unravel the layers and messages within each film.

Of course, there will be individuals that are a mixture or a crossover of each style, but it is important to understand which category you tend to lean towards. Having said this, it is a great time to be a filmmaker as the independent film scene has grown exponentially over the past ten years, thanks to the giant streaming empires like Netflix and Amazon Prime Video. This has opened up a window of opportunity for filmmakers of all sorts, regardless of your style. This is the best moment to obtain an outlet for your original creations.

Tell Your Story

Next, we move on to preparing your idea and script direction. Ensure these two imperative questions are answered:

1. Why do you want to tell this story? and

2. Why are you best fit to tell this story?

Why Do You Want to Tell This Story?

Establish the reason you want to tell your story. What is the message you want to illustrate in your film?

Entertain, Educate or stir Emotion are the three E's to remember throughout the journey of your project. Anything that has become successful or viral encompasses one or more of these aspects in their formula. Upon deciding which of these three E's will be incorporated as the undertone of your script, it's time to dig deep. Get ready and be willing to put in the work; be prepared to see your creation come to fruition as there will be bumpy roads ahead. This means you will be invested: Emotionally, physically, and sometimes, even financially. Never forget the reason(s) why you want to tell this story.

With every character you write and direct, you will need to thoroughly think through every little detail focusing on how every part of the script fits in together to make it a whole. The ability to envision these characters as real individuals interacting with each other will enable the development of multifaceted and profound characters driving forward the message of your story.

Why Are You The Best Fit to Tell This Story?

Ensure you answer why you are best fit to tell this story? Do not underestimate the simplicity of this question. It is a very common question every filmmaker should be ready to answer, yet it is much harder to answer than one may anticipate. The answer is because it is YOUR STORY and you know it best! You have got to believe in yourself. Confidence is the key. As there will always be unplanned instances or surprise obstacles, you need to know that you are the best man/ woman for the job. This is your vision and there is no other person that will tell it better than you. Do not focus only on one aspect of the film—like the script, the characters, or the lighting. You have to remember that filmmaking is about the whole picture. It is all about how it all comes together, and you need to be aware of all the moving parts. Any doubt on your ability to complete the project will chip away and destroy the project, as it will be reflected in you and then, your team. When in doubt, just sit back and know that this is your vision, your idea, and your film and you are the best fit to tell this story.

First Film Notes to Keep in Mind:

- Don't be too hard on self after first one

- Understand that there is no such thing as a perfect film

- Keep in mind that audiences all have their own opinions

THE SHORT-*AGE*

Short films (shorts)

What does this mean?

By definition, a short film is any motion picture, not long enough in running time to be considered a feature film. Typically, the run time for a short film would be 20 – 40 minutes. Creating a short film now-a-days is the best bet for the first-time filmmaker. While there is nothing wrong with developing a feature film, there are so many advantages to first directing a short film before you go to a feature film. Completing a short film will lay out the groundwork for you to create a proof of concept (P.O.C). As you are in the position of finding the type of director you are, you will be able to see the film through and learn from the mistakes much sooner with a short film. In addition, aiming to raise money for a short film will be a much smaller target than a feature film. Even for seasoned filmmakers, in order to raise enough money for a feature film, oftentimes, a proof of concept "P.O.C." shot in the form of a low-to-no-budget short film is employed. This gives producers a taste of your vision. It presents an image that will warrant the confidence in your idea to invest their money into your project.

Short films can go a long way when determining what type of genre of script you like and the type of director you are. Short films are a cost effective way to learn and practice the art of filmmaking. This will serve to find different techniques for filming, framing, lighting, editing and in turn, give you a rough idea of a budget estimate for future films.

It goes without saying that if you speak to five different filmmakers, their comments on short films will vary. They'll either love it, hate it, or refer to it as their early and humble beginnings. Personally, I started with short films, and I still enjoy making them. Bottom-line is that they are mini experiments that can be submitted to festival circuits and used as a pitch for fundraising.

The days of filmmaking with only expensive equipment and large budgets are long gone. If the most expensive camera you have is your phone, then that is great. It will suffice, as it is all you need to get started. If you have a DSLR (this will be covered in a later chapter) or any other higher-end camera, that's a bonus.

Nowadays, you can shoot any type of film on a mobile device like your phone. Most modern phones typically feature standard spec, such as a built-in camera; a built-in light and built-in microphone. These are all the basic equipment you will need to get your project started. Having said that, if you can invest in a portable light or small external microphone to attach to your phone, make sure you do so because it will elevate your production value exponentially and your editor will thank you.

To edit your phone-shot film, you can use existing video editing apps, typically pre-installed on your phone. With this, you can experiment with different features on how to edit your film. If you feel that basic apps are not enough, there are hundreds of additional downloadable apps with upgrades out there. InShot, Adobe Premiere Rush and Viva Video are apps that would work. These extensions will allow you perform more intricate editing, access to manual settings and drag-and-drop files when editing. You will be able to drag-and-drop free preset music files to add to your video edit, as well as free transitions and color filters. The possibilities are endless. With your little portable device, it will quickly help you discover what type of film genre you like and what type of filmmaker you are.

Now, what's next? Go shoot! Go Edit! Shoot more, edit and repeat!

When you shoot, experiment with different angles. Change up the elements and you will discover which angles or settings you prefer. Only by taking action and going out to shoot will you discover lighting techniques that work better with certain subjects and objects.

Use your preliminary shots as your test shots. When they are done, you can go to your editing tools and choose which shots you prefer over others. As you get more experience, you will gain more confidence, allowing you to write and film one or two-minute skits. Involve your friends, round some people up and start shooting some more.

You will only get better when you take action! All the talking and reading will only take you so far! The best way to learn is to just *DO IT*.

"THE BEST EDUCATION IN FILM IS TO MAKE ONE."

- Stanley Kubrick

Once you're happy with a few of your edited clips, find a platform to publish them online. Ask people for their opinion. Show it to friends, family and industry professionals. Survey and see what they think. Bring that feedback to the table. See what works and what doesn't— what you like and what could be improved. Apply the corrections and advice for the next shoot. Most importantly, this is where you will start to develop your style. Don't cave in so easily. Understand that every director and filmmaker has their own flavor and creative eye. For example, Quentin Tarantino and Martin Scorsese have two very completely different styles of work, but they're both very highly respected filmmakers for exactly that. How they portray the script, characters and scenes have become their individual identity. That style and essence is what you will begin to infuse in your work as you mature. It will become *your way* and the truth is, there is no right or wrong way of filmmaking.

"I DIDN'T GO TO FILM SCHOOL, I WENT TO FILMS."

- Quentin Tarantino

Since genre trends change at high rates, a major advantage with short films is that you don't have to play catch up. If you factor in the time it takes to develop an idea from script-to-screen for a full feature (on a low-to-no-budget), you may be a few months too late to catch the trend train before completion. In other words, when you were writing a *Romantic Comedy,* it was the genre of the season. However, by the time you were ready to screen your film, the trend may have moved onto *Sci-Fi genres.* Short films give you the ability to write, film and showcase, resulting in valuable feedback at a much faster turnaround speed.

As a short filmmaker, you will be able to create a flurry of short films and launch them online, which may also land you paid gigs, such as wedding videos, promo videos, music videos and even feature films. All my low-budget-films have been a great calling card—a low risk investment that led me to multiple paid jobs. In my early days, my action shorts landed me two directing gigs: An action feature and cut scenes for a major video game. Ultimately, my work led to additional directing opportunities that include documentaries, commercials and music videos for major sports brands and high profile events like FIFA World Cup 2014.

<u>Showcasing Your Work</u>

Think of short films as a *visual resume.* You have the power to create, promote and screen your project. It will be added to your list of completed bodies of work to showcase your *track record.* "Where do I showcase shorts?" you ask. Remember that *Shorts* are a niche. It is a tool many people can use to measure your potential. Platforms such as YouTube, Facebook and Vimeo are perfect to use as an online portfolio. Do not forget to use LinkedIn to promote your work. Many industry professionals use that platform even more than Facebook, Instagram and Reddit. Also, make sure to use all the right hashtags when you post, to increase your chance of getting noticed in the niche you are trying to attract.

Many film festivals have short film submissions every year, including Cannes. In today's world, there are also many streaming services that accept short films for their libraries and playlists, including Amazon Prime, iTunes, Google Play store and Kinoklik.

Chapter 1

THE CREATIVE: REBORN

> *"You're only given a little spark of madness. You mustn't lose it."*

> — Robin Williams

When you think about creativity, great names like Mozart, da Vinci, Steve Jobs, and Walt Disney come to mind. What do they all have in common? They were all pioneers in their fields and applauded for their innovation, contribution to their industry and ultimately the legacy they left to the world.

Evidently, we can see that creativity exists in all shapes and forms. It can be found everywhere around us. While we can't all be a Mozart or

Walt Disney, we need to always be open to making the impossible possible. We need to have that vision and proceed to capture it one step at a time. Like all other creative activities such as painting, music, acting, dancing and a wide variety of others, we don't have to be masters, but we can engage in them to awaken the creative flow. Creativity is essential to filmmaking and will come in handy throughout your journey. *Our creative attributes once awoken, can help us solve filmmaking obstacles and adapt to situations on the spot. It is this type of creativity that makes solutions oriented filmmakers.*

Creativity will help you reach your target audiences. The world around us is saturated with so many media outlets and by applying some creative thought, you will be able to reach your market on different levels. The use of visual messaging is the key, as many platforms rely heavily on these images to capture attention of viewers. Social media, print and television commercials are great for promotion, but are also a convenient way to showcase yourself and your work. Be sure to create images and videos just for these platforms to connect with your market.

Whether it is to promote you or your work, a mobile phone is an excellent tool to capture the images and create the content you need. When devices like the tablet or smartphone first came out, it was seen as a device for passive consumption—like watching movies and browsing the internet. However, these devices have evolved to be much more than that. There are excellent apps for creating and editing photos, videos, music, documents, slideshows, etc. Ensure you take advantage of these tools. With a phone at hand in this day and age, it is possible for anyone to start creating content.

Creativity is within all of us. Remember the old days of coming up with games to play? Or things to do when we were bored? We need to tap into our playful and innocent selves, where our mind had no boundaries and anything could be possible. As we grow up, society teaches us to be realistic and place boundaries and guidelines with things we do. Our creative genes are suppressed and become dormant over time. You need to invoke those creative genes again. Innately, we are all Creatives. Go back to childhood days and see the creativity we put into our toys that would entertain us. We may have put voices to our dolls or action figures, come up with scenarios or problems with our stuffed animals, created scenes or buildings with our Lego sets, or banged on pots and pans with a spoon to make music. The point is, it didn't matter what we were playing; all that mattered was that we found imaginative ways to get there. Filmmaking is the same. When we hit obstacles, or find ourselves in problems that arise at the last minute, we need to be imaginative and creative to find different ways we can possibly solve the issue.

> **"THE CREATIVE ADULT IS THE CHILD WHO SURVIVED"**

> \- URSULA LE GUIN

My story was no different when I realized at a very young age that I wanted to become a performer. I loved to write. I loved to act. I loved to turn people's frowns upside down through entertainment. Growing up in a war torn place writing the next chapter was an escape that kept me going. Bringing the writing to life gave hope and entertainment through a tough time. I took to writing and creating stories based on cartoons and real life events to come up with the craziest concepts. To this day, I still revert back to my nine-year-old self, and it is through that little boy's imagination I continue to fuel my creative passion.

Although at the age of nine, I wanted to record my ideas, but we didn't have a camcorder. It wasn't until my early teenage years did the first cell phones emerge. Unlike today, these early cell phones were digital and definitely did not have a camera, let alone video. In the early 2000s, I bought a consumer camera off a shelf without any exposure to film school. First, I dabbled around to figure the equipment out until I could take great still photos and videos. Then, I went out to film day and night, exploring and pushing the limits of the camera. Finally, I decided it was time. I wrote a script (inspired by true events), gathered some friends, briefed them and everything else was history (more on this film later in the book). Nowadays, you have a free gift in your pocket, so make sure you get out there.

Heck, with the camera-phones we all carry now, we carry a mini *Hollywood Studio* in our pocket. They are no longer phones with cameras; they are cameras that are phones. Therefore, my lucky friends, this is the perfect time to make movies. Don't worry about what it's going to take. Start thinking about where you want to go and all the resources you may have, no matter how small. Don't doubt or second guess and focus your end goal. Take one step forward at a time. Just SHOOT IT!

Ready?

Take a deep breath...Rolling camera...*and* "ACTION!"

Chapter 2

THE WRITE IDEA

One of the first steps for filmmaking is having a vision, an idea or concept to expand on. Then, bring it to life. Make sure you write it down as raw as possible; no over thinking or trying to perfect it from the get go, just write it down! You can polish it up, trim the fat, and tweak it in whichever way later. Once you start to shape up your vision on paper, you will have what is called *THE FIRST DRAFT*.

Every great film will always start with a first draft and you must communicate your vision with your team, but we'll get to that at a later chapter.

There are so many different programs you can use—like Celtx. Not only is it free, it also provides you with an easy preset layout that will help you with your screenplay, characters, dialogue, screen direction and scenes in a professional manner. I personally used *Microsoft Word* for my first few scripts. I figured as long as people knew what was happening and who was saying what, we were good to go. In the industry, a general rule of thumb is, one page of script is one minute on film. Sixty pages are about Sixty minutes on screen.

When starting, you can take occasional breaks from writing, especially if you're working on multiple scripts. Do 15 to 30 minute increments if necessary. Step away and get back to it with fresh eyes so you don't feel overwhelmed. *Try setting a thirty-minute alarm on your phone. Every time the alarm goes off, do a few push-ups or jumping jacks, wash your face, step away for a water break—just take a break.*

WHAT I DID:

Script development and writing is not a sprint; it is a marathon. Remember to pace yourself. When I started to write my first script, I tried to have it all complete within a few days, no breaks. I would just sit in one spot and write all day long, not stopping for anything except food and sleep. I was committed to my story and vision, and all I wanted was for the script to be done. It was my top priority to ensure that the team collaborating with me would still be available by the time the script was complete.

It was then I realized the importance of breaks to avoid writer's blocks. I realized when the mind is exhausted, the creativity slows down and productivity eventually comes to a halt. Before you know it, your ability to think clearly or stay motivated dissipates. You must remember the value of quality over speed. Furthermore, I realized that just because I may have finished the script or was ready to move into pre-production, I needed to be considerate of other team members and their schedules too. Oftentimes, they may not be available immediately.

During the early stages of writing this first film, I thought committing 4-6 days of the week to writing the script titled, "The Dark Side: Rise of Darkness", for a few weeks would suffice. However, I realized that to truly capture the essence of my story, there was much work to be done and more time would be required to complete the script. I recognized that creating great story is a long process and to master the craft of writing is an ongoing journey.

Initially, the first draft of Dark Side was completed by late 2008. In early 2009, I had already gone through five, completely revised drafts. It was through this time I spent writing, I eventually realized this script was evolving from a short story to a feature length film. By this time, I began to see that my initial idea of a perfect script doesn't exist. There was no such thing as a completely finished script before going into production. Aspects from all facets of the script were ever changing. Anything from character changes, to scene changes, to dialogue, would constantly be revised. In fact, even during filming, revisions were still made throughout.

Eventually, I made peace with the fact that the script's direction would be rewritten multiple times. Depending on each stage of production, there would be different views infused into the story. For instance, the focal point of the director will differ compared to the cinematographer or editor when creating a film. Thus, various input and ideas will be brought up, and many changes will be made throughout the project.

When the script was completed, I took a small misstep of having my friends and family read it. Don't get me wrong, sharing your work with your loved ones is great, but you should be mindful of the feedback they provide as they can unintentionally give you biased responses, stemming from a subjective perspective. In other words, they could overvalue the quality of work because they love you so much, or under-appreciate the task because they do not understand the industry. Aim to have people in the industry with ample experience read your work. Film school teachers or professors are always great to approach. Honest and straightforward actor or writer friends are amazing as well, since they won't be afraid to rip it apart and help rebuild it. These individuals will provide the most valuable feedback and constructive criticism that will help you move forward. Reaching out to people for feedback is also a very good way to create awareness for your work. It helps to create excitement and willingness for people to join your team down the road and eventually bring your vision to life.

As the years passed and my experience grew with writing and filmmaking, I made sure I reviewed my scripts multiple times before I sent them out. I also started to use screenwriting programs with default formats that made it much easier for everyone to read. After your first few films, you will get the hang of it and it will become more of a cookie cutter formula.

Protect Your Script

As soon as you are happy with the final version of your script, you should think about registering and copyrighting it. There are several ways to do so and you should do some research to find out when which method is the best fit for you. Be it a local copyright office within your vicinity or an online process, be sure to understand how it is working to protect your script. I would say the priority of what to copyright goes to feature film screenplays. If your shorts are being used as a *proof of concept* "P.O.C.", which can often be used as a "visual pitch" for investors to help fund it into a feature film, then I would wait until the feature screenplay draft is complete to register.

Now that you're done the script, you are ready to move on to casting, location scouting and gear prepping to shoot your film. Don't fret when you hear someone talk about *money*! Although money is a word that can stop any creative person from imagining, speaking or implementing their creation, you will find out how this can be made possible very shortly.

Money, Money, Money!

Money has brought many people (including myself) to a halt. When people asked me how we were going to make money, pay people, or pay for permits, it made me realize, although we may have it all on paper—the characters, the locations, camera angles and equipment—it doesn't tell us how we can proceed and with WHAT MONEY? This is where you put on your resourceful *"MacGyver" hat* on and get ready to make it happen.

It is impossible to have zero cost on a film. Even if it's just money on coffee, gas or electricity for your laptop to write your script, there is some sort of money that will be spent. Everything has its value. You need to be able to recognize it in all its forms. You may have cast and crew volunteering their time from their paying work to help you out; or you may have a piece of equipment lent to you that would normally cost money and all this has its value. Be thoughtful of these aspects.

You will recognize the values in each facet of filmmaking when you recognize the solutions and methods on how to save that money.

If you would like to understand and get into the money and producer side of things at some point during your filmmaking journey, it is very important for you to remember that finance and budgeting is a huge topic and specialty on its own. As a filmmaker, you will realize that you are an entrepreneur with business making decisions. When it comes to low-budget-filmmaking, you will be wearing multiple hats. You could be the director, producer, and writer—all at once.

I'd recommend when you get to the serious business side of filmmaking, you set up an LLC or INC. This would involve more than one person you trust in the business that guarantees you will not "run and gun" with anyone's money. That is a conversation for specialists in the finance and law side. Please look it up, ask an advisor and make sure you have a solid team to support and educate you.

Hint: Low budget films can often pull money from crowdfunding campaigns, such as indiegogo and kickstarter. This may help you with operating and revenue streams.

"Don't write what you think people want to read. Find your voice and write about what's in your heart."

- Quentin Tarantino

Chapter 3

LAYOUT & STORYBOARDS

Once your script is complete, the next step is to create a layout for the entire script. A layout is divided into two sections: 1.) A list of items you need to shoot your video, and 2.) A storyboard used to guide your shots. You should have a layout and storyboard for every scene in the script. It is a list of items you will need. This could include, camera gear, props, type of location, wardrobe, lights, food, etc. Make sure you determine and categorize the list into what you **NEED** and a list of what you **WANT**. Anything that is not a need will be cut off the list. This will enable you save money and resources and work within a low budget.

The great Wizard of Hollywood, Robert Rodriguez, created the great *El Mariachi* that grossed over $2M in the box office from a mere $7000 production budget. One of my favorite techniques from Rodriguez that

I often refer to is his minimalist layout list. According to an interview (T.Ferriss, 2016) Rodriguez was able to keep the production budget so low with the use of the layout list. He first establishes what he has available and incorporates those items/locations/props in the film. Specifically, he developed a list of items and places known to him from his immediate connections and used them to reduce the cost of production. If he knew a friend that owned a bar, the bar was on the list and later used for a scene. Another friend owned a coffee shop and that location was also on the list and it too was eventually used for a scene. Rodriguez carried this minimalist technique throughout and wrote the movie around all that was available to him. As a result, it gave him the ability to eliminate costs that would normally be associated with obtaining these items.

STORYBOARDS

Together with your list, you will need to create a storyboard for every shot. A storyboard is a visual representation of how your video will be shot frame by frame. It is in the form of a grid-like set up with sketches depicting each shot. Ensure to include notes and directions to accompany each square of your storyboard (refer to table 1.1) A storyboard is necessary for every scene in your script.

This will require a lot of sketching. Nevertheless, the good news is you don't have to be an artist or graphics designer to have a functioning storyboard. Remember, the purpose of a storyboard is to portray a clear vision of your idea to the team. As long as the sketches are clear and notes are concise, you don't need to have immaculate drawings. Most of the time, the storyboard is only seen by your core team. So, even if you draw stick figures with point form notes of what happens, it will be enough. Example of standard points your notes should include are where it happens, when it happens and who is in every scene.

Storyboards are also used to reference while location scouting, on set when filming, and even useful when editing. Having a storyboard will keep you organized and in the long run, save you a great deal of panic. It will help ensure a smoother shoot day and general guidance of your vision, even on occasions you will need to improvise.

After completing the storyboards, use them to establish your shot list and prepare to make an initial requirement checklist. Be sure to include items such as location, camera gear, sound gear, lighting gear, crew (including you), talent and wardrobe. If you've checked all or half of the above list, you're off to a very good start.

WHAT I DID:

For my first few films, I personally drew out every character in a scene on my storyboards. I also made a list of what else was needed in the scene and the location the characters were. I tried to have it as accurate as possible, ensuring the frame and angle was noted so I could refer to them on the day of filming. On the day of the shoot, all I had to do was match the actors to my drawings and communicate the references to my camera team and capture my footage. Eventually, the storyboard was also used as a guide for my editor in post-production.

Hint: Storyboards aren't just great for you as the director, but it will also help your team and performers see your vision before you even film it.

It can be used to help you sell your ideas efficiently when talking to potential investors or producers.

PROJECT ____ PAGE _______

SCENE #:	SHOT #:	SHOT SIZE:

SCENE #:	SHOT #:	SHOT SIZE:

SCENE #:	SHOT #:	SHOT SIZE:

SCENE #:	SHOT #:	SHOT SIZE:

SCENE #:	SHOT #:	SHOT SIZE:

SCENE #:	SHOT #:	SHOT SIZE:

SCENE #:	SHOT #:	SHOT SIZE:

SCENE #:	SHOT #:	SHOT SIZE:

Chapter 4

CASTING

As a filmmaker, the pre-production step is tremendously important. In television and film, a casting (or casting call) is the selection process of who your performers will be—actors, dancers, singers, background performers and other extras that fit a particular role or part in the script. In the low-budget-film world, that also applies to your crew, also known as your "core team".

> **"Casting is everything. Getting the person that you imagined is this character and then seeing what they bring to it."**

> \- Steve Buscemi

First rule of casting when it comes to your low-budget-film is, have your core team. Within your circle, figure out who your core team consists of (at least half the team) and make sure you are familiar with all the different skills each one possesses before you cast the actors.

Ideally, you want to be able to have separate people in all the separate positions; a "specialist" of each department—like an editor, stunt coordinator, writer, sound person, director of photography, make-up artist and location scout. As nice as that sounds, expect that you and your team members will be wearing multiple hats often when creating a low-budget-film. You could be a writer and director. A director of photography and also the editor. An actor and stunt coordinator or a make-up artist that will also do hair and wardrobe touch ups. As the director and captain of the ship, try to have at least another two or three major skills under your belt so that you can step in to help if someone had to leave the set early or booked a paid gig, leaving a gap in their department that could impede the film's progress. You can do this by always taking any opportunity to learn. Be hungry and jump on any chance you may have to work with people in the industry especially the ones in different departments. The more you can absorb the more you can apply to your film when the time comes.

Once you've got your core team assembled, let's move to actors, commonly referred to as *talent*. Personally, I prefer to go in this order: Family, friends, film schools, social media then agencies.

FAMILY & FRIENDS

A popular path many first time filmmakers take is to use friends and family as actors. It is a very cost efficient (usually free) and convenient way to cast and recruit crew for your film. Friends and family will often be very supportive of your project.

Although casting family and friends is often a preference for the first time filmmaker, beware that sometimes, the level of work and professionalism may be affected. Be careful that the lines of fun and work are not blurred. For instance, they may feel like it's a "family gathering" rather than a film set, where it's okay for them to be half an hour late, but in actuality, that could affect the availability of other cast, crew, or how long you may have permission to use a location.

In most cases, family and friends may not be professional actors, so be ready when the movie screens. Your viewers may judge the people on screen. A bad performance could be a quick turn off for the audience, therefore it is a choice you must have to make at your own risk.

FILM SCHOOLS

A great place to find very talented individuals is film school. You have a one stop shop for roles both behind and in front of cameras. Quite often, they will be eager to learn and glad to help for the experience of actually applying their education. Sometimes, being involved in a film project could also be part of their graduation requirements; to shadow a filmmaker or actor on set. This helps them understand the craft in close proximity and in *real-time.* However, students may be inexperienced and could lack the knowledge and confidence in execution, which could result in slowing down your production.

SOCIAL MEDIA

Social media is a great platform that is widely used by students, up-and-comers and professionals alike. It is also a very efficient way to spread the word if you are looking to fill positions for crew and cast.

Thanks to the age of social media, it is largely accepted to respond and apply for jobs online than it was a decade ago. You also have the potential to simultaneously reach a large audience worldwide with a push of one button, giving you access to a body of their work that could be useful for your selection process. It's a BONUS if they have a large social media following that could be considered as a potential outlet for marketing when the movie is complete. The downside to social media casting is that you may not have quality control over the applicants and their portfolios may have altered images or bodies of work, which can be deceiving.

AGENCIES

It goes without saying that going through a talent agency increases your odds to meet and cast high-quality candidates. They usually have access to a large roster with pre-screened skills, characteristics and looks to fit your film characters. They would also typically have them in non-union and union talent groups.

Dealing with agencies is the most expensive choice of casting. There could be many more hoops to jump through, questions and requirements about your project from the agents before being able to audition or cast their talent for your film. The good news is, you are guaranteed a certain quality to be delivered, and if someone "drops" or is a "no show", then expect a replacement.

> *"Casting sometimes is fate and destiny more than skill and talent, from a director's point of view."*
>
> - Steven Spielberg

HONESTY & COMMUNICATION ARE KEY when casting. Make sure to state what the actor and crew will receive in return for their time outright. Don't just post it under "unpaid or non-paying". Be transparent and honest. Please, don't use the word "for exposure" or "it could lead to paid work in the future", as it is overused and often connotes a standalone project with no real growth.

Hint: When hiring your team, make sure to establish if you want to work with union or non-union crew and talent. If you do use union members, you will have to make sure to review each union's requirements, how long you can film and how long you can use them for. Approved union permits will be necessary before filming. There are special permits that could be acquired for low-budget-films and student-films.

WHAT I DID:

The easiest route I took when making my first film was recruiting friends and family as this was the most cost efficient choice. As I got better as a filmmaker, I started to hold *"real"* auditions and made less mistakes with the new team of *professionals.* I also learned the difference between union and non-union actors. For first time filmmakers, you may want to go with non-union actors because of the complexity of the system. I took the non-union route to avoid any additional costs. I discussed all the project details and character breakdowns with all prospect talent, as well as any plans for post filming, like film festival submissions and screenings.

Hint: Always use a breakdown when casting for actors.

Hint: Always provide a breakdown and job description for crew positions.

Audition Breakdowns

A breakdown is a sheet that contains all the important information about your film, for roles being cast.

Sample Audition Breakdown Sheet:

Key Dates, Rates (paid or non-paid) and union info

Deadline for Submissions:

Auditions: (methods *selftape, zoom, in person,* or locations)

Shooting Start Date:

Shooting Finish Date:

Pay Rate and Union:

Storyline and Comments

Storyline:

Additional Comments:

Submission Instructions:

Characters for Movie

Sample character	(lead)	Gender	Age	Scenes
Sample character	(principal)	Gender	Age	Scenes

Chapter 5

I-O-U

Alright, you've got your cast and crew together by this point.

Let's talk about what compensation your team will be getting for being involved in your project. After all, this is a commitment to you and your vision. They are investing their most valuable asset—time. Make sure you are as genuine, transparent and efficient as possible when discussing your methods of compensation. Start by communicating every project detail as much as possible such as where filming will occur, when you will need them, what's expected of them and most importantly, what's in it for them! Make sure that you communicate and settle what will be offered before their first day on set.

Besides us discussing food as a minimal means of compensation, talk with your potential cast and find out what roles they may have always wanted to play and not had a chance to play or be cast for yet. It can be a very intriguing factor when it comes to your project. Example: If someone has always wanted to play a cop, but is always typecast as a *biker,* your project could be that opportunity where they could finally play that *cop* role they've been yearning to book. If the role already exists in your script, you may be able to cast them for the role immediately. If the character isn't readily available, perhaps you may be able to add that role in for them.

You may also be happy to know that many cast members will be happy to volunteer their time on these smaller projects in return for face time. I don't mean *face time the video call app.* I mean a chance to be seen on screen, which is a rare opportunity for most actors when they start their acting journeys. Every actor that's starting off yearns for that few seconds of on screen time. They also need that to build their reels and resumes, especially if at some point they will seek principal agents for representation.

The same goes for your crew behind the scenes. Find out what department your team members may have always wanted a chance to work in and offer them that position or a shadowing opportunity to learn when available. It is very common within the stunts, camera, lighting and editing departments to have new crew member's shadow experienced crew to learn the trade.

There are multiple forms of compensation that can be paid to your talent and crew through one or a combination of the following means: Transportation, food, film credit, footage for their demo reel, and distribution percentage (if there is an intention to obtain a distribution deal). When I first started in the industry, there were many compensation terms I had to learn:

1. **Working for "exposure",** (the overused term) is one of the "work for free" terms. This is a means of compensation that sounds attractive to new actors and crew members with very little or no experience, hoping to gain valuable experience from a specific project. It is generally associated with free labor, so be very selective and really look into the project if offered this type of compensation. Check out the people on the project and determine if it is a fit for what you want to do before committing to it.

2. **"Time For" (TF),** generally referred to as Time For CD/DVD/Blu-ray/online link, which meant in return for their time in front or behind the camera, they would receive the footage on a disc with shots, clips on it, RAW (unedited).

3. **On Screen Credit**, credit that is visible on screen can be seen during the opening or end credits.

4. **IMDB Credit**, credit on the Internet Movie Database (IMDb). This is a searchable database of film industry individuals and IMDb works as an authority that verifies bodies of work.

5. **Food**, meals offered to cast and crew during the time on set.

6. **Travel Fee** (gas/bus/parking), money offered to offset travel costs incurred by the cast and crew getting to and from set.

The most common form of payment for low budget or student films often include the On Screen Credit, IMDB Credit, Food and Travel Fee. Regardless of what you may be offering, be sure to discuss, list, and agree on the terms prior to shoot day. Have it documented and sent over email for confirmation. This serves as an electronic agreement and is a good idea to have a hard copy printed out for reference purposes.

If the intention is to obtain distribution and you are using this as a form of payment, be sure to outline any percentage on the agreement prior the first day of filming. If you have access to legal assistance, that is wonderful. If you don't, at least, ensure you have this outlined in a document dated and signed by both parties acknowledging the percentages.

Keep an open mind when discussing, hiring, and assigning responsibilities as low budget films don't always offer monetary compensation. It is not uncommon that people may challenge you from various departments. Be assertive and stick to your vision. This is a great time to test your people's skills and see if you can take the pressure. Welcome the feedback, praise or criticism, and advice from others, but ensure you stick to your plans and don't make rash changes without first thinking it through. That being said, there are odd cases where someone could be extremely egotistical, negative and self-centered. This may affect the productivity and morale of the team and cast. Avoid this situation by recognizing the red flags ahead of time, and don't cast them for your project. If you have already started filming them, communicate with them in private. State the issue, and if there is no compromise or resolution, let them go.

ALL ABOARD!

Now that you have your cast and crew ready, make sure you communicate and confirm the location, date and time. Make sure you or a dedicated team member have all the schedules, call sheets, shot lists, scripts and all other necessary material printed and with you on set at all times. Upload the information online via Google Drive for ease of access and as an additional backup.

WHAT I DID:

When I had the idea of making my first film, I gathered family and industry friends I met while working on set to share my vision and asked for their participation. I also specified any compensation offered, which at the time was food, partial travel costs and HD 1080p quality footage for their demo reels while offering an amazing learning opportunity. I encouraged everyone to voice any requests for other particular roles that would benefit their reels. For my stunt performers, I asked them if there was a stunt they have always wanted to perform, and I did my best to incorporate that move in the action scenes. If someone from wardrobe had a new clothing line and needed more awareness for their products, then we made sure there were close-ups or the leads were in these new clothing items. Of course, the film credit and IMDb credit were a granted bonus for everyone on board.

By doing this, I established some great friendships over the years that I re-casted for future projects. When the time came, I made myself available to return the favor when they needed me for their projects.

Hint: Always communicate to cast and crew what their positions are before filming.

Hint: Do not assume anyone will want to wear multiple hats or take on a new position.

Hint: Make sure your schedules are flexible and customized around your cast and crew's paid day jobs.

Hint: Deliver the footage as soon as possible for their reels when the movie is done.

Hint: Make sure there are enough and extra copies for all your team members

Hint: Invite your team to any local screenings and do not be afraid to share the good, the bad and the ugly.

Hint: Filmmaking is a lifelong journey of relationships. Who you meet now could be the next top directors and actors.

Chapter 6

LOCATIONS

Locations are a make or break for your film. On big productions, it is a complete and fully fledged department on its own. It bears equal value to the film as writing, editing and casting does. Similar to casting, if you cast the wrong actor to play the wrong character, it could affect your film. Scout a variety of options based on your scenes and script. Rule of thumb, always have an option A and option B (backup plan).

Try and scout both indoor and outdoor locations that require minimal modification. Noise is an issue you may encounter, be mindful of your locations' surroundings. If you are filming outdoors in high traffic locations such as parks, downtown areas, beaches, sidewalks, etc., timing and scheduling will play an important role in your planning. The sound isn't just traffic or people, but it could also be waves, birds, insects, construction, trains, cars, airplanes and tower clocks. Try and learn the patterns, see if there are dead times when you can film or airplanes flying above are irregular at a certain time.

Weather is another huge factor. Outdoor shoots are fun because they offer open spaces surrounded by nature (which you can flip the camera around multiple times to make it look different or bigger than it really is). Remember, you are at the mercy of nature and its elements when you select this type of location. The weather may start one way, then change half way through your shoot. Make sure to plan accordingly by checking the forecast before filming and preparing for any sudden changes in the weather. Hope for the best but plan for the worst.

Hint: The sunlight's intensity changes throughout the day and cloud formations cause overcast resulting in light inconsistencies.

If you are filming indoors, the advantage is that you get to control the lighting, elements and weather. You can light it up in whichever way necessary to keep it consistent. You also have the ability to mimic the elements. For example, it's common to use a fan or leaf blower for wind effects. Fog machines, snow machines, and even custom sprinklers can be used to simulate different seasons while filming indoors. Indoor locations have a different type of noise you must consider like: foot traffic and chatter. In buildings such as schools or offices fax machines, telephones, fridges, fans, toilets flushing or elevators could affect the audio when filming indoors. Once again, see if there is a pattern or a schedule with each location that will be optimal or slow for when you film. Do your research of the items you may need, such as extra lighting. Take reference pictures and communicate with your lighting and camera crew to see if they can work with the location as is. It is highly recommended if one or both could join on the location scout.

When making a list of indoor locations on a low-no-budget-film, the first free location you could always use is your home. Your home can be used to film several scenes and you could use different rooms for different looks. Ask friends and family members if they own or have access to locations such as cafes, restaurants, offices or stores that can all come in handy as film sets. If they are trusting and willing enough, they could also allow you to use their *Vehicles* as *picture cars* (any vehicle driven or parked in a movie) as a bonus!

Reaching out to many small businesses such as family owned bars, restaurants and cafes is a great start for first time filmmakers. Business owners often like the extra traffic, appreciate the business (especially if you buy all your lunch from there) and if you give them a credit or feature them in the film that is often enough for them to let you use their space. Sometimes, you could even have them sponsor the food and location in return for additional marketing opportunities.

THE KEY IS TO ASK OR THE ANSWER WILL ALWAYS BE *NO!*

BE POLITE. BE PERSISTENT. BE HONEST. AND DON'T GIVE UP AFTER TRYING YOUR FIRST LOCATION.

Remember that it's ideal to use a privately owned location of your relatives or friends. Time limits, restrictions and the need for insurance are flexible. You also want to be able to shoot with minimal interruptions. Make sure to confirm the location with all owners. Always be punctual and respectful of time/duration agreed upon and communicate with all parties necessary for the day of the shoot. Always clean up after your filming is done.

Take note of how many people and what will be on set the day of filming. For instance, cast, crew and equipment should all be accounted for. This will enable you to utilize the space efficiently, because you never want to be too crammed or have too much space that you can't fill. Check to see if it will be a difficult location for people to travel to. If so, try and find an alternate location with easy access, to avoid extra transportation and lodging costs. Alternatively, you can re-cast local people closer to that location.

Do you need permission?

The advantage that comes with DSLR cameras is the fact that they are compact, light and relatively easy to move with over full production cameras. You can very easily board a bus, ferry, or enter a mall to grab a few quick shots you need for your film. Does it break the rules? This can be argued both ways, but that's what *guerilla filmmaking does.* Many filmmakers say that unless there is a sign saying 'keep out!' or 'No Photography!' you should be able to get your shots without any permission.

Be sure to familiarize yourself with the rules and regulations of the location you plan on shooting in. Check their website, talk with the owners or communicate with other filmmakers that may have used it to film in the past. When possible, confirm permission to shoot at locations prior to the day of filming to avoid possible setbacks, especially if it's filming near a private or military facility.

WHAT I DID:

We almost got arrested...

In 2012, I was one of several actors on a low-budget-film set. We were informed that we'd be filming a chase scene on a railroad. We drove around a fenced area where there was an opening in the fence parallel to what seemed inactive train tracks. We all walked onto the track side through the opening in the fence, and were cautious of the "live" third rail which often pumps out 600 volts of electricity. One touch could electrocute or potentially kill us. The camera was handheld by the cinematographer, who was also co-directing. The camera rolled and at the end of the take as the director called "cut", a police car pulled over by the fence. A sheriff walked over to us and ordered us to step away from the track. He informed us that a passing train had reported us and what we were doing was extremely dangerous and completely illegal as it was considered to be trespassing. After asking for our IDs, he notified us that our actions would warrant a hefty fine or an arrest. The director took full responsibility and apologized for his behavior. To this day, this experience ranks as one of the top close call adventures that we have and it will live on to be told for many stories to come. With this in mind, there is a saying that "it's easier to ask for forgiveness than ask for permission" which is very true with low-budget-films, but when you are responsible for others, choose the safer bet.

ALWAYS PLAN B

"Remember that sometimes, not getting what you want is a wonderful stroke of luck."

- Dalai Lama

When I was filming my first movie back in 2008, one scene got completely written off last minute because of a flood four hours before call time! The location was a nightclub that we were able to secure for free. On the night before filming, I was rehearsing an action scene with two other actors until 3:00am (four hours from call time). This scene had a call time of 7:00am with a total of **110 people** scheduled to be on set at the same time. This was an extremely important shoot as it was one of the final climactic scenes in the film.

Now before we move on, I would like to pause for a second to consider how hard it is to gather and schedule 110 people at the same time. Picture what it takes to organize and call a meeting for 10 people that <u>must</u> attend and now multiply that by 10.

Getting back to the story, our rehearsal was going smooth and everyone was excited. At 3:30 am, we received a dreaded call that the location had flooded! Our first response was how can the location flood? Secondly, we looked at what we could do to make it possibly work. Our key challenge was how to notify and reschedule the 110 people that were scheduled to shoot on such short notice. Social media wasn't as commonly used to communicate and keep everyone posted and there was no real reliable method to mass connect with everyone to notify them of the news. Additionally, it was a horrible time to call as it was so late in the night.

After several calls with the location coordinator, we were told the entire venue was flooded because the main water pipe had split in half. Everything from the floor, furniture, DJ equipment, lights, electrical wires, and hardwood had water damage. Once it was confirmed that there was no salvaging the shoot as planned, we had to reschedule and proceed to contact all the people. We had to have broken some sort of record that night as the other two actors and I quickly called, emailed, left voice messages to every single person on the list.

That night, I learned a harsh lesson that anything can happen even with the best of planning. Through this incident, it taught me not to take anything for granted and to always plan for things not going as planned. Be it an unexpected accident at the location or a sudden weather change like a snow storm midway. Always have a plan B.

Location Checklist:

1. Is there a cost?

2. Is there power?

3. Where are the breaker boxes?

4. Is there noise?

5. Is it near traffic a major intersection or airport?

6. Is the neighborhood safe?

7. Is there a place to use as a holding, catering or setup area?

8. Is there parking?

9. Are there any other events scheduled in or around the location?

10. Are there bathrooms?

Hint: Always have extra power sources like batteries or portable generators when filming.

Hint: Always make sure you know where the closest hospital is in case of emergency.

Hint: Always rehearse before the shoot if possible to maximize your time on location.

Hint: Ask for a part of the location if the whole location is unavailable when filming.

Hint: Think creatively and see if you can use the location you will film at for different scenes. Maybe each corner can be used as different sets for your film

Hint: Always make sure to ask if there is a maximum capacity for people on site.

Hint: Always have another scene planned in case the first one doesn't work out.

Chapter 7

TRANSPORTATION

Transportation is key to making sure that your cast and crew are able to get to and from set. You will most likely have to arrange for transportation (shuttle, uber, taxi, or carpool) costs of cast and crew. This could include fuel and parking, if crew members drive their own vehicles and make long trips back and forth during production.

When shooting on a low-budget-films, your best bet is to "hire" a local crew and cast to avoid these additional expenses. If you have to choose non locals for your team, you will need to discuss fuel expenses with crew and cast beforehand. You may be able to charter a shuttle van or bus to pick up people from certain *pre-arranged* spots around the city. For example, a major intersection downtown or a mall uptown.

Big budget features have an entire department dedicated to **Transport**, with a full team of coordinators to oversee transportation requirements for film crew, talent, background performers and the stars. You or an assigned team member will need to create a pick-up and drop-off schedule and communicate it with your cast and crew.

WHAT I DID:

For my films, we mostly used the car pooling system. We would first identify where our team members lived and arranged to pick them up directly from home. If not, we would pick them up from a major intersection on our way to the film set. If the car was packed with gear or people, we would sometimes have to make a second trip.

Hint: Make sure your team communicates with you or the driver of the shuttle when en route.

Hint: If possible, arrange with team members to carpool with other crew or cast members if they reside around the same locations.

Hint: When running late, always communicate with your team.

Hint: You may be able to get a street side parking permit for the fraction of multiple parking permits.

Chapter 8

ACCOMMODATION & HOLDING

Where your crew and cast are going to stay is a common question when planning your filming schedules, especially if you will be in a location that is considered 'out of town' or remote. To avoid any last minute stress during pre-production, make sure you communicate with your team if you will be arranging for any day or overnight stays at a local hotel, motel or base camp near the filming location. If it is within driving range, your talent and crew may be able to drive back and forth daily as long as you compensate them for gas or transport. Nowadays, *air bnb may* be a cheaper alternative to hotels, which could possibly be used to house the entire team and used as a location to film.

Holding or "green room" as it is often called on film sets is an area designated for talent that are on stand-by. It is very common that on low-budget-film sets, tents, canopies or cars can be used to *hold* cast and crew, especially during outdoor scenes when it could get extremely hot or cold. These holding rooms may also be used as a changing room for talent, used as a storage for gear or a food area. Make sure to communicate with your team to clarify any questions about Holding.

WHAT I DID:

On set, I would always have a dedicated area for holding, catering and gear. If it was not possible, we would use our vehicles to assign different cars for each purpose. For example, red car had camera gear, white van had food and the grey car had props. For my next few films, I bought a portable changing tent and a camping canopy, so that we always had a changing room separate from the holding area, which also doubled as shelter from heat and rain during outdoor shoots.

Hint: If you are filming in a location that is similar to a house or warehouse, it is common to set one of the rooms as the green room. Quite possibly your hair, make-up and wardrobe departments may also be able to set up a mini area to prepare actors in other vacant rooms not used for filming.

Hint: You may also use one of the rooms or kitchen when in a residence for catering.

Hint: If there are any extra rooms, they could also be used as rehearsal rooms.

Hint: Make sure you follow and apply all COVID-19 safety rules and regulations.

Notes:

Chapter 9

FOOD & CATERING

Food is a key necessity for your cast and crew that will keep the team happy as they work hard on your film. It is the minimum compensation requirement that may be a deal breaker if it is not offered for team members that are volunteering their time for your project when you have casting calls out. Nothing can ruin a good shoot more quickly than a hungry team or bad food.

The first thing when considering feeding your cast and crew is an initial head count. You will need to set aside a budget for food or make sure you have a family member or friend that can cook for everyone. Figure out who and how many people will be on set each day. Some days won't require having the whole crew and cast. Once you have your head count, it is advisable to take note of any food allergies or food restrictions. Everyone that has worked on a low-budget-film will tell you that at one point or another, the food on set was pizza. As with previous points, check to see if you have any friends or family members that can provide you and your team with food if they own a catering business or restaurant. It is possible to work out a deal with a location you may be filming in or nearby i.e. restaurant or cafe scenes. You can usually work a discounted rate on the location, if you purchase drinks and food for the team filming on the location. Another way that works is, if we will be in the shooting area often, we ask for a 'bulk' discount, and we guarantee to purchase our lunch or refreshments from the said cafe or restaurant. If you're really lucky, you can get it for free, depending on the value you will provide the owners. Food is an essential item on your film checklist and is the most basic form of *compensation* under the *"work for footage"* standards.

WHAT I DID:

When filming my first few films, I had made a few deals with restaurant owners that we would be purchasing food from them for the next few days, which got us a major discount when ordering. On other days, I also ordered several pizzas, subway sandwiches, Chinese food, Vietnamese soup and homemade catered food (from friends). I made sure any allergies or food restrictions were cleared with the team before placing any orders. Coffee runs were on a daily basis.

HINT: When ordering bulk food, make sure to try and have it in separate containers or limit how many slices of a pizza each person can have, so there is enough for everyone.

HINT: Always mild and spicy on the side.

HINT: When filming for multiple days near a cafe or restaurant, negotiate with the owner for a discount on your orders.

Chapter 10

CAMERA, LENSES & LIGHTING

CAMERA

The ultimate question every filmmaker will ask is what is the best camera for filmmaking?

The real answer is, what is it that you currently own without any additional costs?

These days, it is almost impossible to buy a bad camera, especially with all the tech that is retrofitted in cameras. If you can afford a particular camera and additional lenses, that is a bonus! Make sure to choose your camera and lenses wisely, based on what type of film you are filming and what type of filmmaker you are. Are you looking to move around a lot or will you just mount the camera on a tripod?

Besides using your cell phones for filming as an incredibly cost efficient camera, Low-budget-filmmakers may want to purchase an affordable camera that can deliver quality. Here's a few things to keep in mind before your next camera purchase:

Video Quality: Make sure you buy a camera that offers great quality video. Most cameras nowadays have amazing quality, 4k resolution capability and at the very least, 1080p Full HD. This is probably the least of your worries. I suggest any camera that can shoot 1080p or higher would suffice.

Low-Light Performance: As a low-budget-filmmaker, you'll probably find yourself filming in many low-light situations. It's always a good idea to choose a camera with a large sensor and higher ISO (the way a camera senses light) to help you perform well under poor lighting conditions.

Ease of Use: It's essential for every filmmaker to be able to control the camera and access your settings easily. Find a camera with a user friendly interface menu, especially if you're a new filmmaker.

Battery Life: Every filmmaker has to factor in how long the battery life is for the camera, according to their usage. If you are shooting longer videos or in harsh weather conditions, it's essential to understand that you will need multiple batteries as backup, which is something to consider for your budget when buying your camera.

Lenses: Most cameras come with their custom selection of lenses. However some cameras may have interchangeable-lenses and are compatible with various models. Be sure to factor in the cost of lenses when purchasing your camera.

Image Stabilization (IS): The majority of the cameras out there and some lenses can provide the option of image stabilization, which reduces the camera shake during your handheld and walking shots. Some camera bodies and lenses will be equipped individually, and when paired, result in a smoother and clearer video. Although not necessary, it may come in handy if there will be a lot of motion in your film.

Autofocus: When you are a new filmmaker you will realize that autofocus could be a very useful tool to have. As your filmmaking skills improve, you may want to move on to manual focus.

Luckily, as a filmmaker, you have tons of budget friendly camera options that can deliver great quality. On the other hand, if you don't have access to a camera, most current phones shoot at least 720p-1080p (DVD/Blu-ray quality), and others can even go up to 4k or shoot in 3D. So the next time you are ready to dive into a camera purchase, ask yourself if your phone is good enough.

WHAT I DID:

I started by using my cellphone camera to frame shots and record some video tests. I wanted more control over what the camera could do, so I used the family's *point and shoot camera.* It was a simple yet efficient way to learn the basic differences between contrast settings, autofocus, manual focus and shutter speed. Eventually, I borrowed a few friends' cameras to film a 15 minute test short film while discovering a plethora of different options and utilizing a swivel screen like no other cameras I've used had. Eventually, in 2007, I made the decision to buy my first DSLR camera and shot my first films on it.

Hint: Test your camera or camera phone in different surroundings and before you film.

Hint: Most cameras, much like eyes, will see what you want it to see. You need to make sure there is enough light for it to capture the video or image you want it to.

Hint: Have a shot list for your shoot. It will help keep you on track for framing and time. *A shot list is a detailed checklist of shots that you need, want or plan to take on the day of the shoot, usually given to the team and camera crew.*

Hint: When filming, shoot-to-edit. Shoot every scene as if you are editing in your head. Also, get extra shots (time permitting). If you have extras, it's better to not need it, than need it and not have it when editing.

Hint: When filming in cold places, make sure to have extra batteries as the cold will deplete the batteries quicker. Also, make sure to give some time for the camera temperature to adjust to avoid any moisture from building on the lens or internal body.

Hint: Make sure to have gloves if you plan on hand holding your camera outdoors in cold locations. You may be able to find fingerless or flippable gloves specific for camera operation.

CAMERA ANGLES

When you start filming, you will realize that sometimes, different angles will help you tell your story better visually. That will all come down to your choice of camera angle and how much you balance what you capture of foreground, background and your subject. Here's six, basic camera angles you should familiarize yourself with:

1. **Establishing shot:** This is your introduction to your setting, story or character.

2. **Wide Angle:** The lens is either zoomed out completely or categorized as a "wide lens", which will help you see the widest view possible. Many establishing shots are shot from wide angles. They are great to show the entire location, or environment you are showcasing.

3. **Long shot:** You see the entire body of a person; head to toe. The subject will fill the frame entirely from top to bottom. Such shots are great for action, such as running, dancing, fighting or character introductions.

4. **Medium shots:** The camera will see the top half of the subject—typically waist up. This is great when filming basic action or dialogue.

5. **Close-up:** This is usually a shoulder or half shoulder and head. You could also leave some room above the head so it doesn't look like an extreme close up. This is employed when you're trying to capture eye and facial expressions of your subjects.

6. **Extreme close-up:** This is where you really go up close to your subject's face. No room above the head and less shoulder than a close-up. This will really show intensity in the eyes, lips or facial expressions. Typically, it can be edited to cut back and forth between close-ups and extreme close-ups.

Before you get to the chaos of being on set, take your camera for a spin. Experiment with your camera and shoot from different positions and angles. Try to film from above, below or at eye level of your subject.

Next are the supplementary filming angles that can be used in combination to your basic angles:

1. **Two shot:** The simplest setup for two people in frame for dialogue and basic interaction. Both people are in frame and can be done as a long shot, medium shot or close up.

2. **Over-the-shoulder:** When two people are facing each other during a dialogue scene, place the camera over one of the character's shoulders and focus on the other person who is speaking. In the frame, see the back of the head or a part of the shoulder of the person closest to the camera. Then switch the camera over the other person's shoulder and go over the other character's dialogue while keeping a similar framing as the first.

3. **Dolly:** The dolly effect makes it feel like the camera is on wheels and moving closer or farther away from the subject. Using wheels, a track, a portable dolly or simply a skateboard, office chair or towel on a table that you pull slowly across a table will all have a gliding-moving effect for the shot.

4. **High Angle:** Shooting your subject from a higher angle than your subject. A modified bird's eye view. This angle can make a subject look shorter, smaller or weaker than they are.

5. **Low Angle:** Shooting from a lower angle than the subject with the camera pointing up. This will give a more dramatic or hero look.

6. **Dutch:** Slightly slanted camera angle that gives the audience a tilter point of view. Many filmmakers use this angle to add suspense, evoke tension or a psychological meltdown to a character.

Subject-to-Camera Positions:

It is important to determine the position of your subject-to-camera to accurately depict the mood of the scene.

Front: A head-on frontal view is as though we're looking at the person's face and eyes directly. Make sure to specify if your actors should look at the camera or off to an angle when using this angle. Audience is more engaged when used.

Three-Quarter: Shoot off center. You should see three-quarter of the face, half profile-half front. The audience is less involved when used.

Side View: Side profile shot. The audience is more observing when used.

Back View: Shot from behind them, and can be over one of the shoulders. The audience can feel the character is upset or vulnerable.

WHAT I DID:

For my first film, I just used a wide lens for every shot I had planned. I moved closer to the subject, or further away from the subject—all with the one lens to capture the angles I needed. Ultimately, I learned that you shouldn't do that unless that was the only lens you have. The subjects looked warped, I lost detail in my frames and I had limited frames overall to edit. So, I sold the lens in exchange for a zoom lens halfway through filming. The zoom lens was definitely an affordable alternative for capturing a variety of angles, including wide and tight shots. I also learned afterwards that the footage frames per second (fps) rate did not match the editing rate. The result was an unwanted trail like motion blur to every performer's movement on camera. It was a lesson well learned to always make sure the frames match, unless you shoot it at a faster rate, for the sake of slowing it down in post (for a slow-motion effect). Lastly, when filming scenes in dark areas, I increased the ISO to compensate for the darkness. It created an undesirable grainy effect that had lost much of its detail.

Hint: Check your video settings before shooting for frame rate: When shooting video for a cinematic look, use 24fps—for a television show look, stick with 30fps. It gives a better and smoother feel for live TV.

Hint: Over the shoulder cheat (When shooting with only one camera). To save time for dialogue scenes between two people, you can set up the camera at the 180 degree angle or over the shoulder facing the first actor while both actors go through the entire dialogue. Once done, reverse the camera to the other actor's 180 degree angle or over the shoulder and have them go through the entire dialogue again with the focus on the other actor. You can cut between them in post. I would recommend a master angle where you can see both of them in the same frame. That means you may have to shoot the scene three times.

Hint: When shooting on your phone, always shoot landscape 'horizontal'. Try avoiding portrait 'vertical' positions.

Hint: If you don't have a tripod to hold your camera or phone, you can use books, tape, shoes, pizza boxes or coffee mugs to lean it against.

Hint: Make sure to playback what you just filmed before you move on. Check the video for focus and lighting when you play it back, preferably on a bigger screen than the one on the camera for accuracy.

LENSES

Lens choices play an essential role when capturing your scene or subject on video. If you are able to get your hands on a camera such as a DSLR for the shoot, then ideally it would be good to have at least two or three different lenses; one that can give you a close up, another that can give you a medium and a wide-angle lens. If you have a close up lens only, you will be limited to a certain distance and look when filming. Having a wide lens such as a 28mm wide-angle will provide you with a different look and will allow you to see more than the close up lens. You may be able to crop some of the frame in editing; keep in mind that this may result in some loss of quality. If you can find a lens that is more sensitive to light that would be great—a plus such as a 50mm prime lens could work. Your equipment can grow as your skills mature.

Hint: Consider a camera that comes with a lens kit when you are starting your gear collection.

Hint: Most kits come with a zoom lens, your next buy should be a 50mm prime (non-zoom) lens.

Hint: Prime lenses will usually give a higher quality and more 'cinematic' look to your scenes.

Hint: Make sure the lenses you purchase fit your camera, or you may need to purchase an adapter.

Hint: Wide lenses are great for real estate and establishing shots, not close-ups.

Hint: Many phones have lens kits that allow your camera to shoot wide, macro and fisheye or increase zoom capabilities.

Hint: Always clean your camera lens before shooting, no matter how clean it may seem.

Hint: If you can only buy one lens, get a zoom lens to be able to get a mix of wide and tight shots.

Chapter 11

LIGHTING

Lighting can easily make or break films. It is what sets the film's visual mood, atmosphere, depth of field, era and ambiance that will connect the dots for the audience with every scene. Most filmmakers will focus on the camera, lenses and angles, but without the lighting, the video will lack quality.

When working with light, keep in mind the direction, quality and contrast of light. Figure out what your basic light sources are—such as sunlight, candles, flashlights, work lights, vehicle headlights or even in some cases, moonlight. Take note of what is already available on-site and what you will be bringing with you to the set. The lighting setups will vary based on the sources of lights. It is important to know what look you want to portray when filming.

Quick Lighting Setups:

Practical Lighting: When the light source is visible on camera and is used as an in frame object and an active light source that will illuminate your frame or subject.

Three Point Lighting: Is a basic setup with three types of lighting in three distinct positions to light up your subject; a key light and two filler lights facing the subject. An easy way to remember the setup is, the Key will be the main one your subject faces. The Filler and Backlight are on your left and right side to help light your face or subject and help eliminate shadows while creating depth. The exact positioning of the lights may vary, depending on your requirements.

Natural light is awesome because it's free! Yet, you have to consider the fact it could change in a heartbeat, and on a consistent day, you could get about half a day of sunlight, that's where you hear "we're losing daylight" as many Assistant Directors hassle everyone to get moving and on track when things start to slow down.

To save valuable time, I would recommend the director of photography or lighting team go into the location (during the scout or before the shoot on the day) and test out how it will look like on camera so when the talent is there, you know exactly how to shoot and where the light sources will be positioned.

WHAT I DID:

I used many daily items such as lamps, work lights and portable single bulb stands to light up our scenes and subjects. My team and I also used bed sheets to diffuse any harsh lights and aluminum foil to bounce light onto low light areas.

Hint: You can mount flashlights in shoes, hangers, against books or tables to light your scene when filming.

Hint: Avoid shining a light directly downward or directly upward on a person, unless that is the desired look.

Hint: Use a diffuser to avoid harsh lighting on your subject

Hint: Test all your lights before you shoot. It is not advisable to have different tones of light on the same subject.

Hint: When using hot lights or candles, make sure they are placed at a safe distance from plastic or flammable objects.

Chapter 12

SOUND ADVICE

A film school professor once told me that sound is 90% of film. We can all really just see one picture at a time, but we can hear dozens of distinct sounds at the same time.

Sound is incredibly important because it is what engages the audience when watching your film. It helps fill gaps and deliver information to your audience's brain. It is what tingles our senses, speeds our heart beat and stimulates emotional responses. Have you ever watched a scary movie without the eerie soundtrack? It doesn't have the same effect, right? Yet, if you covered your eyes and could still hear everything, you still felt scared. That's because of the soundtrack and sound effects' ability to stimulate our senses. Similarly, fight scenes may lose some intensity without the impact sound effects and sitcoms may miss on comedic timing and humor without the laughter soundtrack.

Even though film is a visual experience that tells a story through motion pictures, the sound makes scenes memorable. It is what weaves together the story by setting a mood and evoking specific emotions from the audience to the points they are supposed to feel them, especially where no traditional narrative is present. There is something visceral about the emotions that we experience from music, that when combined with great visuals, creates a truly immersive experience.

The more films you create and the more films you watch, the more you will realize how some films are supposed to look grainy. Others are supposed to feel like a home video, for example, *The Blair Witch Project* or *Paranormal Activity,* but the audio is always great quality. Generally, sound is divided into multiple segments. Dialogue, sound effects, soundtrack and licensing.

Dialogue

This is the speech between the characters played by the actors on your set. It is very important that you remember that dialogue recording clean audio is just as important as recording a clean video. This will save you the headaches of redoing poor audio after wrapping.

Dialogue can be captured using multiple methods. You can use a boom mic. A shotgun mic, a combination of recorder and mic or even the internal camera mic. When setting up your microphone, make sure you place the microphone 6-14 inches away from your subject. Always make sure someone from the sound department checks your levels. Usually, between -18DB and -6DB is the best range for sound.

Lastly, when it comes to editing, take the time to level out and clean up all your audio tracks and make sure the sound effects and music you add accentuate your work and not overpower your dialogue.

Now that you understand the basic importance of sound, make sure you have a sound person on set to record dialogue and room tones too. Make sure you or the sound person is good at it, to avoid any disappointment and extra work later on.

WHAT I DID:

The first film I created taught me a very valuable lesson; that audio is extremely important. My team and I were so focused on the camera, the lenses, the video quality, the script and how the actors performed, we left sound quality at the bottom of the list. Eventually, we learned that bad sound (especially when filming outdoors on a rainy day) was a disaster in the editing room. It was near impossible to salvage and use any audio without the use of additional in-studio recording. From then on, the audio and sound department became one of the top priorities when filming. To ensure we captured the dialogue clearly, we created a DIY boom pole (a pole that holds the microphone on the end closest to the speaking actors) by attaching our shotgun microphone to one end of a 12' paint brush extension handle ($12) with an XLR cable that connected the microphone to the camera and it worked like a charm. Saved us the full cost of a real boom pole priced at $150.

Hint: Try to set up the mic in an area that doesn't limit the talent's actions or performances.

Hint: Always make sure the boom mic is out of frame.

Hint: As your filmmaking matures, do some research on lavalier (lav) mics, stereo mics, single tracks and multitracks for audio recording.

Hint: Shotgun mics are extremely versatile and affordable for filmmakers. They often come with an indoor and outdoor mode to help with echoes and noise filtering.

ADR recording

Automated Dialogue replacement is the process of re-recording dialogue. The original actors (or replacement) redo some of the lines to improve the audio quality. This process is often what saves many films from poor audio. ADR provides you the chance to recreate the moment from when you were on set in a quieter, more controlled environment. But, it comes at an inconvenience and a cost. It is ultimately up to you to decide if your film needs it when editing.

If you don't have access to a studio, find a quiet and enclosed room at home and get ready to hit the record button. Nowadays, you have amazing phone apps that allow you to record crisp quality sound, saving you time and money.

WHAT I DID:

After learning the importance of audio, I always have someone in charge of sound when filming. I rarely rely on the internal camera microphone when using a DSLR, as they tend to pick up a flatter sound and the camera's internal noise which affects the quality of the audio. When we didn't have access to a studio, my car was our makeshift recording studio for ADR. With windows and doors closed, it became a great soundproof space.

After recording the ADR, we uploaded it to our computer then added all the necessary background sounds for the final edit.

Hint: Always test your locations before filming. Clap, talk, and listen to any echoes or subtle noises that could affect your filming or post production process.

Hint: Always get an external microphone when possible for your DSLR or phone.

Hint: If you have sound proofing panels, cardboard boxes or panels that can help deaden the sound when recording at home, that could be of help.

Hint: A little secret we found that works like a charm when searching for the perfect ADR recording environment—get into a car, close the windows and doors, record and hear the magic.

Dubbing

This is similar to ADR. Dubbing is the process of recording mostly dialogue in the studio. Occasionally, they may re-record sounds to the soundtrack. Dubbing is usually the term people use to translate films for foreign countries in their native language.

Foley is another aspect of sound. Footsteps, breathing sounds, zippers, cigarettes being lit, liquid poured into a glass, waves against a dock or bullets hitting a wall are all examples of follies. Foley complements the sound recorded and can replace actual sounds from the time of filming. The sound you hear in film is often a combination of what was recorded on set and extra sound effects added on. Some of these sounds can be recorded while on set as an add-on. Other times, the sounds are created and recorded in-studio. Similar to soundtracks, Foley sounds can be found for free, bartered or paid for online. Do some research for soundtracks and Foley, and don't be afraid to ask if you come across a sound artist.

*Did you know **Foley** got its name from Jack **Foley**, a sound effects artist who developed and shaped the technique?*

MUSIC

Remember that even though your film is low-budget, you will always need to have permission and clear any permits (written or email copy) for all music used. Just because a song you like is online or used with another video does not mean you can download it and use it for your film, especially if you plan on having it distributed, screened online or at a film festival. Music composers and sound designers can be hired for a fee. Students that want to specialize in that department are also a cost efficient alternative.

In the editing stages, soundtracks can be purchased royalty free online. There are several websites that offer a variety of music. There are many composers that create custom tracks especially for film, and if you ask nicely enough, you may be able to get them to compose custom tracks for a nominal fee. Occasionally, you can find recording artists that want to help on forums or YouTube, in exchange for something as simple as a music credit at the end of your film.

LICENSING

Licensing is a means for music creators to ensure that their work is protected from misuse by others. Copyrights are safeguards for the creator and the creator's team that collaborated to produce the lyrics and sound recording.

Quite often, filmmakers will need three licenses to integrate copyrighted music into their projects. These licenses are:

1. Master license - allows you to use the master recording of the song in the film, but you cannot re-record or edit the music,

2. Synchronization license - grants you the right to edit the music to the video clips in your film and;

3. Print license - you require a sheet music to reproduce the song, even if you can find it for *free* online.

It is very important to secure the proper licensing for the proper terms of use to avoid legal issues.

Licensed music is where several creators come together to produce the lyrics and sound recording, each having to grant you permission to use their work. The benefits of royalty free music is that it has all the licensing pre-negotiated and handled for you. A subscription may be necessary to access the website that can provide you access to thousands of quality songs with a single search. Ultimately, the decision to use licensed or royalty-free music comes down to preference, but for the first few productions, I would suggest the effective and no hassle method through stock and royalty free music.

WHAT I DID:

When it was time to add music to our video edits, I initially just used a variety of songs I had on my computer. However, when it was time to submit to film festivals, we needed to re-edit the entire music track or the submission would be declined. We always made sure to have some form of proven permission to use the music in our film. I had a friend and local band that offered to compose a new track for our film because they wanted a credit in our film. I was also able to browse the internet and find many royalty free websites—just make sure you purchase the correct license (personal, commercial, etc.) to avoid any legal roadblocks.

Hint: Many new recording artists have songs online that they are happy to share for 'exposure' as long as you credit them. Make sure to communicate and confirm with them and have it in writing.

Hint: Reach out to film school students, who could be specializing in music composition.

Hint: Before you use or purchase any music, have an experienced individual review any licensing before you proceed with the editing process.

Chapter 13

PRE-FILMING CHECKLIST

---

o   Story or Idea

o   Write it down

o   Re-read, test and tweak your story

o   Create a storyboard

o   Find a Team/crew

o   Cast your actors

o   Scout your locations

o   Communicate all the above in a briefing with your team

The points above are an easy checklist to the main pre-production stages that should be completed before filming. This is also a very similar process to what a standard Hollywood Movie will use in the early stages. Don't fret if some of these points overlap or happen simultaneously.

Make notes of any additional filming ideas, potential connections for gear or locations below.

NOTES:

____

____

____

____

____

____

HALFWAY POINT

IMPORTANCE OF BELIEVING IN YOUR PROJECT

As you reach the halfway point, you will realize that you may be exhausted physically, mentally and emotionally from all the pre-production work. Your mind may have considered quitting at some point, which is normal with how overwhelming preparing for a movie can be. Remember why you started in the first place, push through and keep your eyes on the prize. Your mindset is the most important asset on your filmmaking journey that you have embarked on. Your belief in your project is as powerful as all the aspects we've covered thus far. In times when you feel stressed and exhausted, or your team is doubting their abilities, your funds start depleting and you can barely afford food for your cast, you must continue to lead. Persevere through your project, find creative ways to make it work and continue to pour your heart into your project. This will inspire actors and team members to go out on a limb for you as they will feel your devotion and follow your example.

The idea of creating and filming your own content, especially for actors accustomed to taking directions and only being in front of the camera, can be daunting. But seriously, it doesn't have to be. The more you create, the more freedom and inspiration you will have.

WHAT I DID:

As a performer and filmmaker, I realized that everyone hits a slow period annually. So, it's important for me to use that time to continue to hone my craft. Either by continuing to practice monologues, studying film scenes and characters or watching movies to inspire my acting and filmmaking. I always make time to write multiple scenes or full scripts to improve my writing skills, performing methods and filmmaking techniques. Ultimately, unhinging myself and taking control of my own creations allowed me to continuously do what I love. Instead of waiting for the phone to ring to book you jobs, you can learn to be the one making the calls doing the hiring.

Hint: The pandemic has provided many actors with the time to start learning more about film production, writing and creating their own content. Use this time as your "off-season" for when the "on-season" comes around.

Hint: Hollywood productions have been largely affected due to the pandemic. Many productions of movies and TV shows have come to a halt, which means there is a chance for independent filmmakers that are creating content to receive the exposure they desire if they provide streaming services with new content to fill the void from the lack of productions.

Hint: Keep pumping content out there, because those in power positions that were always busy have a lot more time on their hands to view more content than before. The odds just got higher.

"There are no rules in filmmaking. Only sins. And the cardinal sin is "dullness."

-Frank Capra

Chapter 14

IMPORTANCE OF REHEARSALS

Rehearsals are an essential part of any film production, no matter what the budget. Rehearsals save time, leave room for little error and save money. The more time you have to rehearse— whether it's with the actors, camera department or stunts—once in production, it guarantees a smoother flow and everyone can concentrate on shooting the film.

When you run rehearsals before the shoot date, you increase the success rate for the actors to deliver the performance you seek. For the stunt performers, you increase the success rates for fluidity, realism and safety. For DOP and Directors, rehearsals help finalize their shot lists, blocking with actors' positions and focus.

Last but not least, time is money. Rehearsals mean more preparedness for you and the team. Work is more efficient when the camera is rolling. If you're renting gear or location, you'll be done in time without the risk of going over time.

WHAT I DID:

I would bring in my director of photography when possible and at least one of the actors to come in for dialogue rehearsals. It was a must because it saved us from doing so on the day of the shoot. It also gave us a chance to discuss any final adjustments for the script and anything technical like angles, lighting or sound.

If we had any action scenes, I would make sure the performers involved rehearsed at least a month in advance from shooting to make it as natural looking and seamless as possible. If we had a gym, we would use that. If not, we would use a park for free or someone's basement if it was cold out. We would also rehearse a few times before we rolled the camera on filming day.

Hint: Rehearsal will increase the performer's confidence when it is time to film.

Hint: Rehearsals help solidify any questions about the script for the actual shoot.

Hint: Rehearsals will allow performers to focus more on the performance part on the day of shooting, instead of spacing and positioning.

Hint: Action and stunt rehearsals will ensure the fluidity, realism and safety of the performers. It will also provide the director of photography with enough time to reference how to capture the action.

Hint: In a time like COVID19, rehearsals prior the shoot day will mean there are fewer people occupying the space when crew are trying to set up the set for filming.

Chapter 15

ACTION & STUNTS

Action and stunts for film are one of the most unusual and difficult feats for anyone involved. The performers require skill, accuracy and training. The camera department needs to understand how to capture the artist's physical performances and the editing departments need to combine all the parts and sometimes even enhance it by Computer Graphics Imagery "CGI".

There is a misconception about stunts we need to clarify before we move forward. When people think of stunt work, the first genre of film that comes to mind is action. *Mission Impossible, John Wick, Avengers* or *The Expendables.* However, that is not the case. Stunt coordinators and stunt people's jobs stretch across many movie genres, from horror films to comedy. It's just unfortunate that stunt people and coordinator's jobs are often overlooked.

The job of stunt coordinators and performers allow physical ideas written on pages to come to life safely. A simple tumble in a comedy, a jealous push away in a romantic or a desperate getaway in a horror movie all require a stunt coordinator to be part of the movie crew.

The Stunts category is divided into a few sub categories.

Stunt Coordinators are usually experienced stunt performers, current or past, that are hired by a TV, film or theatre director or their production company. The coordinator is responsible for stunt design and stunts performances for the production. Stunt coordinators will arrange stunt performers and stunt doubles casting for scenes that will require *stunts*. Their job description also entails that they ensure the safety of the performers while they coordinate with the rest of the team. The stunt coordinator will often work closely with a special effects team when intricate scenes will include additional gear or effects such as squibs and explosions.

Stunt coordinators will often look at each stunt performer's training when considering casting performers or stunt doubles. Once the hiring is complete, there will be a previsualization "previz" session, where they will most likely be training all the stunt performers during pre-production, as well as any actors who will perform minor stunts themselves, and lead a team of fight coordinators, stunt doubles, stunt players, and stand-ins. All that will be collaborated and reported to the director.

Previsualization (also known as ***previz, previs and previews)*** is the visually mapping out scenes in a movie, commercial or music video before principal photography. Previz helps the Director, DOP, crew, editor and some producers understand what the scene will look like on the day.

Stunt Double is a trained stunt professional, who will replace the main actor during a dangerous or physically demanding scene.

Stunt Performers are trained men and women that are professionals in single or multiple talents such as, precision driving, high dives, high falls, martial arts, skydiving, gymnastics, etc. They can often be seen confronting the main characters or heroes.

Stunt Actors are stunt performers that also occasionally deliver a few lines before performing the stunt. In previous years, there would be an actor to deliver lines then a stunt performer replaced them for the action segments. This new category of stunt-actor is a cost and time efficient choice for productions. It also offers more screen time for the performers.

Action Designer/ Fight coordinator is generally experienced in martial arts and stunts. They will typically take charge of designing a fight. They focus on building and designing every movement, much like a dance choreography. They will also take charge of rehearsing with the actors and teaching them all the movement, like a personal trainer would to help build the physical skills to pull off the choreography. Sometimes, on low-budget-films, the title of fight coordinator/ stunt coordinator will be a one person job. On bigger productions, they will be separate job titles.

Lastly, if you are a filmmaker or performer looking at the different styles of fighting or martial arts disciplines to study or have performed for your next film, there is no *one* perfect style. It is no longer Krav Maga, wrestling, Kung Fu, boxing, karate or taekwondo solely. All the arts are great in their own ways to give you a sense of what the real moves and techniques will look and feel like, but it will most likely not apply the exact same way when filming. Nowadays, action scenes are no longer just *a* single style like boxing. Movies and Coordinators tend to mesh many styles for the intricate choreography of action scenes and performers, which the audience tend to enjoy more.

WHAT I DID:

Fortunately, since I have a background in martial arts and action for film, I was able to fill in the role of the stunt coordinator. I always rehearsed with my cast and camera crew to view the action from beginning to end at least once before filming day. I also made sure the performers and I had tested any stunts that could possibly go awry, to ensure their safety on the day of filming. I gladly demonstrated any stunts that needed a demonstration. If there were any fears or concerns, we had ample time to modify the stunts. On some occasions, while filming, I took over the camera to capture the angles or timing of certain moves when the performers executed them.

Hint: Unless your character is representing a certain style, like a Rocky Balboa (boxing), Ip Man (Wing Chun) or an Eddy Gordo (Capoeira). I highly recommend you attend Action for Film or Stage Combat class that will explain the difference between what's good for real and what's good for reel. As a performer or filmmaker, the classes will teach the best angles, frames and spacing to capture the action for film.

Hint: You could also look at the different styles between the Hong Kong Style, which focuses on the performers doing most or all the action at a certain complexity, rhythm and pace with very little cheating on camera.

The choreography is very much like a dance with a lead and follow. An action and reaction that could all be captured in one or two takes. Hollywood Style tends to focus on expressions, close ups, quicker cuts, and reverse angles. Camera shakes and quick camera movements are often incorporated to intensify the choreography. Whether it's one or a mix of both styles, if you are a beginner, remember it is sometimes easier working with someone with no real training and working with them from a basic level, than someone with former training and trying to un-train them.

Hint: If you will be capturing the action on camera, watch some action movies as references to see how they capture the action. Every DOP and Director like to capture it differently. You may want to capture some of it handheld and the other part using a tripod. Make sure to rehearse with the actors and capture many angles when you first start shooting action. It is COMPLETELY DIFFERENT than shooting dialogue.

Hint: When filming action, make sure you advise your performers to focus on technique, even if it means going slower with the action, which could be sped up in post. There's no fixing bad technique in post.

Hint: If you, your director of photography or performers are new to action, make sure to rehearse before filming, and capture as many angles as possible for post. It is better to have extra angles and clips than wishing you had them.

GUNS & FIREARMS

A common question about guns in film is, if they're real. In general, some films and shows will certainly use real guns, especially for camera close-ups, but never real bullets. The real guns are often modified before filming and some are modified to fire blanks. Almost all scenes with guns in holsters or when a gun is not being fired, prop guns are usually used. They are lighter than the real guns.

The main firearms rules that have to be established when on set is to treat every firearm like a real loaded firearm. Don't fool around or point it at anyone (unless it's part of a rehearsal). Finger always off the trigger, and if you're required to have it on the trigger for a scene, make sure to take your finger off when the director yells "cut". Don't drop it, sit on it or stick a finger in the barrel. Keep in mind that blank rounds can kill, and guns that fire blanks get hot after firing.

You as the filmmaker should take every reasonable precaution to protect those working with you as firearms increase the risk of injury.

WHAT I DID:

When I needed guns for the films, we asked friends to see if anyone had BB guns, airsoft guns, toy guns or props that came with Halloween costumes. All we had to do was spray paint them black. We made sure to inform any neighbors or people walking by that this was a film project, and not an actual situation, to avoid any panic. We posted signs, distributed letters to nearby houses and made sure we had a few people from set communicating to curious onlookers. When using the guns, we tried to limit how long we had it out for, and when possible, tried to use it on private property only. As I matured with filmmaking, I always had a paid duty police officer to make sure we don't run into any legal roadblocks.

GUN WRANGLERS

Gun wranglers (armorers) are licensed firearm professionals that have to be present when using replica or real guns on set. They take full control of the weapons before and when the scene is done. From their arrival on set, they debrief production, actors and stunt players of the scenes the guns will be involved in. They are responsible for the dispersion, and checking (before and after each use) locking, cleaning and storing of the firearms. Some wranglers may be able to provide your production with the gun rental services.

There have been several film sets I worked on where a paid duty police officer was on set when the use of firearms, explosives and uniforms was required. To avoid any confusion or delay in your filming schedule, you must notify your location owners and local police service if you intend on using special effects, firearms and pyrotechnics.

GEAR & TRAINING

If you are looking to start performing some of the action. Research your local classes for stage combat, action classes and martial arts classes to learn basics. Dance, yoga and gymnastics classes could also help you with flexibility, working with a partner and choreography memorization. Once you have acquired the skills and ready to perform, you will need at least basic stunt gear in some scenes. Start shopping around for prices and buying your *basic gear* if it's within your budget. The basic gear typically consists of elbow pads, knee pads and some form of back protection such as an *armadillo* (priciest on this list), especially when looking at branching into stunts with hits and falls. You can also DIY by using cleaning sponges for knee and elbow areas, wear multiple layers to protect the back and core area, or even purchase dollar store painter knee and elbow pads.

Hint: If you are shooting action scenes on a Low-budget-film, you can always look at using pillows, bed mattresses, moving boxes to pad the floor during falls. If you will be doing break falls (falling down on the floor or onto something), fill out your outfit with sponges, add extra layers of clothing under your costume and if you really feel uncomfortable doing the fall or stunt, always voice it.

Chapter 16

LET'S GEAR UP

Use this chapter like a mini gear checklist before you head off to set. Gear is essential for every filmmaker and as much as filmmakers of all levels generally love to show off their new gear, this is the *essentials list*. Remember that not all gear is essential and if you're starting out, you need to have the basics. What are the basics? Well, if you ask ten filmmakers (including myself) what's in the bag, the results may vary. However, there will be a few things you should find in common. Don't have the money for some of these things? Let's figure out how you can still make it work.

Gear List

1. Camera of choice (Phone, DSLR, GoPro)

2. Lenses to match selection from point #1 (if possible)

3. Batteries and Charger (make sure to charge before every shoot)

4. Memory Card to record all your video and sound

5. Hard drive (external)

6. Tripod (lightweight preferable)

7. Light source (work lamps or a home lamp)

8. Reflector (We've used tin foil or white Bristol boards to bounce light)

9. A microphone to fit your DSLR or Phone (if possible) built-in is fine for starters

10. Tape will be used in at least 100 different ways (multipurpose)

11. An extension cord

12. Flash light (searching and lighting)

13. A computer to upload, edit and share your work

Let's quickly go through why each of the above is necessary.

1. Camera of choice will be your main source of capturing the performances. Make sure to test your phone or camera of choice. Ensure it's operating well a few days to the shoot day. Clean it, remove the battery and pack it.

2. Lenses are essentially what act as your camera's eyes. It will help with capturing the performances while allowing a certain amount of light at a fixed focal point. Some vintage lenses may give you a nice preset tone. There are some great lenses for both DSLRs and phones. You can get creative and shoot through rings, bottle openings or plexiglass for bonus effects.

3. Batteries are the life source to your camera. Make sure you have multiple or aim for at least one spare battery that is always charged. Use the charger to keep them topped up. If you're using your phone, make sure to carry a charger or two in case one stops charging.

4. Memory cards are the storage for everything you will be capturing while filming. Make sure the speed matches the quality of recording. Also, as nice as it is to have one card that is 80GB, I prefer to have 2 or 3 that are 20GB in case one card crashes or malfunctions, I don't lose everything.

5. Hard drives are a must! Back up your work as soon as you can, and try to back that up on another drive, just in case the first one crashes. After all, you don't want to waste anyone's time or effort. Also, make sure to watch your dailies after every shoot on a bigger screen than the one on your camera to make sure it looks good or to ascertain if a reshoot might be necessary.

6. Tripods are every filmmakers must have. You will need them for those steady shots. Don't just rely on your built in stabilizer (whether phone/DSLR). Tripods can also be modified in many ways to cheat a crane shot. When considering the different tripods, make sure it's a fluid head tripod if possible. Photography tripods get jerky when panning. Weight is another factor to consider. The lighter the tripod, the easier it will be while moving around. Also, keep in mind the material of your tripod. If it is metal, be careful as it can get really hot or freeze and either stick to your skin when moving it by the legs or the leg locks could get stuck together.

IF A TRIPOD IS OUT OF YOUR BUDGET—use books, shelves, cups, tape rolls, books, shoe racks, shelves, mugs, bricks or stones to help raise and mount your phones and cameras. Get creative with how you can make it work. You can try leaning it against, in, on or under. Got none of these items? We've placed a shoe on a pile of books and use the shoe collar to hold the camera phone.

7. Light sources vary in power, tones, sizes, shapes and heat. For example, the sun is a great and *FREE* light source. Yet, it can also become overpowering for basic camera settings, extremely hot for equipment, uncomfortable for team members and unpredictable with overcasts. When indoors be resourceful and see if you can get your hands on a lamp from home, single bulbs, or work lamps to start your lighting kit.

8. Reflectors help you to control light outdoors or indoors. They are very easy to make at home, to bounce light onto your subject if there are shadows or dark areas that lack light from one side. You could also use tin foil, mirrors, white sheets or white boards to bounce the light's brightness onto your subject.

9. A microphone, specifically a shotgun mic is a small size microphone that delivers good sound quality. Most can be attached to phones or DSLRs.

10. Tape is truly every filmmaker's best friend. You can use it to anchor down cables, hold together a broken piece of equipment, keep a door from locking, or mark a position on the ground. You could also use it to hold up items or reflectors and tighten wardrobe that may be too loose.

11. An extension cord will come in handy when you need to charge or power up an item especially if you're using a phone that's running low on a built-in battery.

12. Flash lights are great when looking for kit items in the dark, and can often come in handy when helping the camera focus in a dark surrounding. It could also double as a light source to help with lighting.

13. A computer that is compatible with the speed, power and video quality captured from your camera is necessary. It is a personal preference if you like Mac or PC. The higher the quality, the more powerful the computer will need to be. Also, make sure that your internal storage is not overloaded to avoid crashes. The computer will also be used to help you backup your cards regularly throughout your shoot. Editing wise, many computers nowadays come preloaded, with at least basic editing software. Search the market or talk to friends to see if there is a way to share a license for a professional editing suite.

GEAR CHECKLIST & NOTES:

____

____

____

____

Chapter 17

INSURANCE

Low budget filmmaking and guerilla filmmaking typically have been known not to have insurance on their sets. Which means if there is an injury, vandalism or theft, you would be held accountable. Film equipment is expensive, picture vehicles are expensive and locations can be expensive. The insurance needed to cover such costs would have to be researched and selected based on what is on set, where it will be filmed and how many people will be present. This way, you can protect yourself and others if anything were to *(knock on wood)* go wrong.

Insurance also has many different branches under the title. It is an entire subject I suggest you do your research on what is necessary to protect you and your team through the various stages of production. Usually, some of the basic reasons to get insurance are broken down into the following three segments: Legal, contractual and property protection.

LEGAL: Almost all locations and financiers will require a filmmaker or their production company to have some form of insurance, which covers property damage and bodily harm to third parties. Insurance companies will issue a certificate of insurance which will name the location or the financier, which is proof there is insurance in place.

CONTRACTUAL: Part of many broadcasters or distributors will require you to have insurance before any payments are processed. Distributors and broadcasters often refer to this as errors and omissions insurance and will not distribute a film without it. This covers things such as being sued because you used a song in a film and did not pay for the use. Or a coke bottle in a shot without approval of Coca Cola. A lawyer is normally involved prior to approving coverage and they will review the film and make sure all legal clearances are in place prior to distribution. You can buy this insurance during production or when you have secured a distribution deal. The policy can last two years or three years depending on what you need contractually from your broadcaster or distributor.

PROPERTY: They must have to protect against damage and loss to assets, such as equipment that you are responsible for (especially when rented out through a company). Assets are anything that is not an automobile. These policies do not insure against anything automobile related. You need a separate non-owned auto policy for that.

There may be additional insurance coverage that may be mandatory or should be considered when filming in foreign locations.

Film production insurance protects your production company, project and team from related liability, by covering a specified value amount and should be tailored to a production company's needs at the time of purchase.

Non-Owned Auto: When renting a vehicle for use in a production, you need to arrange the insurance for that before you use the vehicle. If you rent a van from Hertz to carry around equipment, you need to have insurance in case you are in a car accident or the vehicle is stolen.

WHAT I DID:

When shooting my first film, we filmed at our own risk. Everything was communicated beforehand, and the team and I assessed the majority of the risk prior to day one of filming. The locations, gear and team were all non-insured. However, I did come to an agreement that if anything were to happen to the location while filming, I and the team would be responsible for any costs of damages. All the vehicles involved in the movie were operated by the vehicle owners only. As for the gear, we owned all the gear, therefore, any loss or damage would be our responsibility. For the second film, I printed and distributed waivers as a cheaper form of waiving any claims while filming.

Hint: During COVID19 shutdowns, there are no insurance companies offering "COVID coverage" for any new productions. Existing productions are currently in turmoil due to any cases that have occurred on their set. (This could change depending on when you read this).

Hint: Always try to insure equipment and vehicles. They tend to be the most claims reported, especially if they are rentals and not your own.

Hint: Your personal car may need additional coverage through your provider if you use it as a "picture car" for filming.

Hint: For more information, check out my friends at marqueeinsurance.ca

Chapter 18

PRODUCTION DESIGN

This step is where you get creative and embellish your set(s) with props, decor and furniture. Many Indies overlook this step, which can make or break the completeness of the scene. It can change the character of an empty room from four walls to a loveable, believable and relatable room. If you have a budget, great! If you don't have a budget, try to use whatever you have at home or pre-existing on the location you will film. DIY and build something from scratch, tweak an existing item, borrow off friends or family, try thrift stores, garage sales or even recycle spots.

PROPS are typically practical items used on screen to help enhance a performance. This is another film item you want on your checklist. See if you can build, create, tweak existing items or get for free (even from scrap or recycle) and of course, through a relative or friend. Oftentimes, you might also be able to get some endorsements or sponsorships for your film in return for *product placement*. Example: A company may offer to give you a case of drinks to place on the counter during a bar scene, in return for everyone identifying the brand next to the main actors or in the hands of the actors in the scene. We were able to get a few stools, a breakaway table, and demo television set for free in return for a *special thanks* in the credit roll at the end of the movie.

Filmmaking isn't cheap, and acquiring every piece of gear or prop you can get for a *feature product placement* will go a long way.

WHAT I DID:

When my team and I needed props like food, we used our actual lunch food for the scene, then ate it after we wrapped filming the scene. Any items like canes, chairs, tables, we used real items around us. There's no limits to creativity, but make sure you have something great for close-ups. My team and I used a plastic poster tube to cheat a bazooka in a wide angle shot, toy guns or knives that we spray painted to match the real colors for action scenes and cardboard shields that looked great. For fake blood effects, we used a variety of mixes that included food coloring, bbq sauce, and even soap. It all depended on how thick we needed it to be. We also used everyday items just lying around the set. Occasionally, even camera gear. Just get creative with what you have as always.

Hint: Make sure to avoid or cover any logos on real-life items you will use as props.

Hint: Strip labels off pop and water bottles or rotate cans and branded bottles so the logo is not facing the camera side.

Hint: When using a prop that is delicate, make sure to inform your actors to treat it as such. If possible, try to film the scene that involves that scene to decrease the odds of its destruction.

Hint: When using real items that could be dangerous as film props, make sure to inform the actors and crew. Example: Chairs, knives, hammers that could be used for camera close-ups.

Chapter 19

COSTUME & WARDROBE

Every actor appearing in your film will need costumes bought or made for them at some point. The costume(s) will reflect the era and genre of the film which will affect the budget. Costumes for characters indicates the time period the film is set in as well as personal traits of the character. Although costume design plays an essential role in filmmaking, its creators are often overlooked. Many memorable film characters are identified by the wardrobe they wore in the film. Iconic costumes like Black Panther, Superman, Batman and Wolverine have lived on for generations and are recognized by viewers of all ages.

Even though a costume designer is the individual in charge of designing and fitting the clothing worn by actors in film productions, typically on low-budget sets, you don't need a costume designer or stylist, instead, you or another team member may have to assume the role of wardrobe. You can ask actors to bring a few different outfits to choose from on the day of the shoot. Make sure the outfits have no logos, text, profanity or novelty on any of the clothing items. For lead actors, you may need multiple identical copies in case one malfunctions. Also, make sure to notify them of where they will be filming so they don't bring clothes that match or blend with the background. For example, not to bring a green shirt on a green screen shoot day.

WHAT I DID:

I asked my actors to bring their own wardrobe for several scenes while filming. I sent them reference photos, and they emailed or text me photos of the different outfit selections they thought fit the preferences. We were as specific as possible to simplify the selection process. For example, if we had a wedding scene, I wanted to see tuxedos and dresses only. For a bar scene, I wanted casual attire only, like jeans and a t-shirt. On some occasions, I would also ask them to bring multiple outfits to set because it is better to have more options than not.

Hint: This is one of the easiest steps when filmmaking. You also guarantee that the clothes will fit the actors.

Hint: You can send reference photos to the actors so they can prepare a similar costume for the shoot.

Hint: If you are shooting a scene and need extra people. It is very common to reuse an actor (especially background performers) and have them change their wardrobe and come back as someone else). This is also used on big Hollywood sets.

Hint: Always notify your actors if there will be any blood, make-up or spillage on clothing items.

Hint: Always ask for options. Better to have it and not need it, than need it and not have it.

Hint: Make sure to do your best on any location you secure to have an area for changing.

Chapter 20

HAIR AND MAKEUP

Hair and make-up is what compliments the wardrobe and completes the actors' preparation stages before going to camera. Depending on the genre of film, role and costume, you may need a special effects make-up artist for blood, prosthetics or lacerations.

Much like any other department, you or another team member may have to fill the roles of hair and makeup.

WHAT I DID:

I had actors do their own make-up most of the time if I didn't have make-up available on the day of the shoot. There was one occasion where the make-up artist could not make it to the set, but she gave me her kit to help the actors apply basic dirt and blood on the actors' faces.

Hint: You may need to send reference photos of make-up for actors.

Hint: Actors may need to bring their own hair and make-up to set, especially if multiple looks are required.

Hint: Make sure you confirm which one or multiple skills your make-up artist has prior to shooting. Example, special effects makeup, hair, or regular make-up.

Hint: Make sure to do your best on any location you secure to have an area for hair and make-up to set up and work.

I THINK YOU

ARE READY

READY - SET - LET'S SHOOT!

You've polished up the script. Know it inside-out. Communicated and assembled your team. You've prepared your plan A and plan B for any tricky **curve ball** *"worst case scenarios"*, such as unreliable weather. YOU are ready to shoot your movie!

If you have followed the tips we discussed and planned correctly, this experience should be an enjoyable, slightly stressful and extremely valuable undertaking. Of course, you will run into a few unforeseen circumstances, and the unexpected usually occurs on film sets, which you can't do anything about except be resourceful and make sure to communicate any changes with your team immediately.

Keep in mind that you and your team will most likely be working longer than usual hours. You will need to be on location earlier than your talent to make sure you are ready to move when they arrive. You will also be the last one to leave to make sure the location is in pristine condition after you wrap and tear down.

You have to find it in you to keep everyone motivated, energized, and joyful, with eyes on the prize. Make sure everyone is safe, healthy and well fed, with occasional breaks throughout the day.

Make sure that you also back up any files to external hard drives. That includes sound, images and videos.

At the end of the day, make sure you continue and finish the project with the same high spirits that you started with. Make sure to acknowledge everyone for their efforts, and treat them all as equals. After all, all the people that believed in you, your vision and leadership are on board to support you and they expect that in return.

WHAT I DID:

When it was time to film, I brought all the positive energy with me and passed it onto my team. I looked at this journey as an opportunity to bond with my team, test my skill and also improve my performer skills. I always made sure I communicated with my team if there was a sense of urgency, and there was time for fun and time for work. I learned that all my work had to be backed up, then backed up again. I also made sure they knew I appreciated each and every one of them.

Hint: It is okay to feel overwhelmed. Step back, take a minute, then go for it.

Hint: Always have multiple memory cards because saving all your work on big cards are tempting but are a complete disaster if they fail.

Hint: Communicate. Communicate. Communicate.

RE-SHOOT

It is not uncommon that you wrap your filming and move into post production, then realize some scenes didn't end up looking like how you'd hoped it would. During odd occasions, you may realize that some scenes may not have even been shot. Don't panic or get worked up about it. Look at the bright side that the main bulk of the movie is done with and in the editing stages. To get a few more quick scenes should be a breeze. Communicate with your team and organize a schedule accordingly.

Trust me when I tell you that you should savor those last days before you wrap up. When filming on set for a period, you create a family feel. You all realize you all have each other's back, and when it's all said and done, you will miss those long days you spent together, making something impossible, possible.

> *"My advice to young filmmakers is this: Don't follow trends, start them!"*

- Frank Capra

Chapter 21

EDITING - THE PIECES COME TOGETHER

Editing your film is one of the most important steps to stitch up all your work in one. All the pieces of the puzzle you worked so hard to attain becomes complete after editing. Good editing can help a movie move at a good pace, establish the story, and achieve the proper engagement with its audience. When scenes are edited well, emotions, tensions, mystery and action colligate in the right shot. Editing is the main key to blending the images and sounds that will make us feel emotionally connected and truly take us on a journey while watching the film.

At an earlier chapter when we mentioned *storyboards*, that is considered one of the initial stages of editing to many filmmakers.

You, as a filmmaker, will often have some shots in mind already, then while filming, you will realize how certain shots and angles will be based on how you envision it in the editing room.

Whether you are editing or have an editor on your team, there are a number of skills you must learn to hone to shape the story and tone of your film.

- **Analyzing** your footage entirely: Every single shot that was filmed must be analyzed. This will help you to decide on how to best achieve the desired emotional and thematic clip for your film.

- **Problem solving** If an actor's performance is weak during a take, you must work around it. Overlay the audio while using another actor's angle or cut to a master angle. Quick cuts for action and sometimes masking (highlighting an area) may be required for poor lighting scenes.

- **Being Detail-oriented** is every editor's strength: Good editors have the ability to go through hours of footage, and choose which cuts will make the final edits down to a microsecond.

- **Communication** with all team members is a must. Editors must communicate all the updates for the different edits, the problems, solutions and the creative decisions to the director.

1. Pace

All of us have seen tons of slow movies. The storyline dragged on while we checked out watches for the end in what seemed endless. It can be because of bad acting, a bad storyline, but usually a slow pace of a film is due to inappropriate editing. Good editing can help a movie pick up the movie where it lacks, and help it to continue to move at a good pace that suits the story line, leaving the audience with a proper engagement. Select what is relevant to the story, important to the action and use transitions that will contribute to the story.

2. A good shot

When scenes are edited well, a mix of emotions, tensions and mystery marry in the right shot.

3. Continuity

The one word that floats around every director, script supervisor and cinematographer on set is continuity. Continuity in a simple editing explanation is when the editor takes all the scenes and puts them in a logical chronological sequence. The beginning, the middle, the end. A skilled editor will make sure the puzzle pieces of the story are seamless and logical.

4. Action

Editing action can be a lot trickier than dialogue. There's a mix of character angles, action sequences, and body close-ups that must be stitched together seamlessly to create an impactful action sequence. The performers' level may achieve the desired results with the least amount of editing. Other times your editor may have to resort to 'quick cuts'. Aside from the action and reaction of the performers or skidding cars, there could also be the use of CGI.

5. Bloopers

Every film set will have outtakes or bloopers. Whether it was someone that walked into frame, a wardrobe malfunction, a microphone dropped on an actor's head or a person started laughing hysterically.

Editors have learned to look out for "mishaps" or bloopers and use partial or alternate clips of each performance. Oftentimes, editors will create a *blooper reel* at the end of the movie with the credit roll or a special category on a DVD featurette.

CLOSED CAPTIONING is a text version of the dialogue parts of a television or movie presented. The difference between *closed captions* and *subtitles* is, it was developed to aid hearing-impaired people while subtitles were intended for viewers who can't understand the language. In the low-budget-filmmaking arena, either are useful for film festival screenings or to aid with poor sound quality.

WOOHOO!

YOU'RE DONE!

FILMING IS WRAPPED. EDITING IS COMPLETE.

NOW WHAT?

DISTRIBUTION?

FILM FESTIVALS?

YOUTUBE?

VIMEO?

NETFLIX?

Notes:

"I thought drama was when the actors cried. But drama is when the audience cries."

— Frank Capra

Chapter 22

DISTRIBUTION

Distribution is almost every filmmaker's dream objective. Distribution is associated with that final step that will help promote, support and showcase all that creative effort and work you put in.

There are many different outlets and platforms through which you can secure distribution for your short films. Remember that distribution could happen at an early stage or late stage of production. Many filmmakers attempt to secure a well-known actor or crew member that may help secure your outlet and provide you a pre-buyout percentage before you film. If you complete your filming and then search for distribution, you may have to do more research to see if your product fits the outlet and if you can reach an agreement. Many low-budget films also go the self-distribution route and organize their own cinema screenings and DVD sales.

FILM FESTIVALS

Film festivals are a great place to showcase your work, find potential distribution, network with other filmmakers, creatives and performers, whether you are new and emerging or a pro in the industry. Besides a great place to showcase your work, film festivals also usually provide seminars to gain new techniques and volunteer opportunities to gain work and industry experience.

Keep in mind that most film festivals have fees to enter. You might also wish to have your cast and crew attend the film's premieres. Remember that these costs are still included, even though the movie has been completed.

Are film festivals still relevant?

Film festivals have always been a place where your work could get recognition. If your work is nominated or a selected winner, that serves as a stamp of approval, which in return could aid you in securing funding for future projects or distribution on various outlets.

Recently, film festivals seem to be more and more at risk since the rise of the streaming and VOD era. Many filmmakers and screenwriters have found instead of using film festivals as the 'middle person' that once connected them with the screening and distributing outlets, that they can now pitch their work directly to many of the streaming platforms. Whether it's as early as the screenwriting stage or a completed movie, creators could now skip the film festival hustle, the laurels, and shoulder brushing and approach streaming platforms such as *Netflix, Amazon, Apple TV or Hulu* directly to get *picked up for* "original content".

YOUTUBE & VIMEO

YouTube and Vimeo are great platforms to upload and showcase your work. You may have tried the film festival circuit and not gotten accepted. You've approached traditional distribution but with no avail, and self-distributing is more costly than paying off. What are you supposed to do now? Put it on YouTube or Vimeo for free!

The competition is very fierce since the digital innovation in filmmaking. This is a guaranteed method that no matter how many other people may have said 'no', you still guarantee your work will be up!

Don't be too hard on yourself. If this is your first movie, congratulations. Expect that your team, friends and family can kick back and enjoy the fruits of your labor—a Journey many will only talk about but never attempt, and best of all, you will be learning very valuable lessons for your next project.

Besides it being a free screening that doubles as a lesson, it will also serve as a promotional tool for those willing to invest down the line. This is also a great way to receive feedback by reading any comments people leave. You can always **TAKE IT DOWN** if you suddenly hear from a distributor that wants exclusivity.

There's no right or wrong for either of these two choices. Based on personal experience, uploading content on YouTube feels like you're a content creator with a following that expects momentum and continual posts to keep your subscribers and viewers interested. Vimeo feels simpler. Even though it may feel that the crowd is smaller when you upload your work, it feels that your audience may be more concentrated on niche films instead of pure entertainment and how-to-videos.

WHAT I DID:

For my first film, my team and I were able to organize a cast, crew and friends' private screening. We worked so hard to have the edit and screening copy complete, we rendered the edit, but the disk would not play! It was a different format than the system at the screen. So we always check what system the venue or theatre you plan on screening has from then on. We also always make backups in case the one we try does not work. After having to reschedule and render a new copy the screening was great, we received invaluable feedback and it was a great chance to see the movie at full size. You really get to see the true colors and hear how the audio will sound in a high quality surround sound system. My team and I made the readjustments and we submitted the film to multiple film festivals. We eventually started to get feedback about selections, nominations and dates. We tried our best to be there as a team to watch our film make its debut in multiple countries. Once we established how the system worked, the rest was like clockwork—you just uploaded the screeners(your film submission) to the festival or submission disks (Blu-ray or DVD) then waited to hear back. Also, remember that some festivals allow you to submit rough edits.

When we were done with the festivals, we reached out to multiple distribution platforms to try and monetize our film. There was no luck for the first seven years as short films were rarely a competition for feature films. The result was online uploads and personal distribution attempts. Luckily, a few years later, a few companies reached out from Europe, United States and Air Flight companies to negotiate our film's acquisition. When we discussed options for pay, it was sometimes part of the contract to remove the films off any other site on the internet until the contacts ended.

Hint: Don't sell yourself short! Know your team's and project's worth and don't jump on the first offer you receive.

Hint: When editing, make sure to use a calibrated screen when possible. The colors could vary from one screen to another and could look completely different when uploaded or screened in theatres.

Hint: Always render a first copy, then test it on multiple devices before screening or submitting your film or uploading it online.

Hint: Remember to render your movie at the same frame per second "FPS" as it was shot on.

Hint: Make sure to label your film accurately and have an appealing thumbnail and title. It will drive traffic and compel people to watch your video.

Hint: Make sure you have a disclaimer and age restriction (if necessary) before your film screens online.

Chapter 23

ROLLIN' WITH THE CREW

As your productions mature, so will your teams, gear and budget. This is a bonus detailed job and crew list for your first budget film, which I hope this book helps you secure. The beautiful part is that, just like with no-budget-films, the key to all the pieces of a puzzle is teamwork. You are interconnected to make one movie happen.

ABOVE-THE-LINE CREW

This crew is your essential team that you will need to assemble, gather or hire before pre-production. On a bigger budget film set, many of these members may be members of unions or guilds and they may also have agents that represent them.

SCREENWRITER

They will flesh out your idea into a full script. They may also need to obtain story rights if you are making a film based on a book, video game or play.

PRODUCER

There are different tiers of producers; some that raise funds, some that engage in quality control and some that can help with organizing the departments.

DIRECTOR

The director is the creative captain that will bring the vision to life.

DIRECTOR OF PHOTOGRAPHY

The DOP or DP is usually part of the next category, but they can be an essential part of the pre-production process. This position can also be listed as *cinematographer*.

BELOW-THE-LINE CREW

Once you have completed your above the line crew, you start to assemble the rest of the team. Your Director and DOP may have a few recommendations of teams they've worked with on past projects and who to hire at this stage.

Remember not to get too carried away on a low-budget-film. The size of your budget will determine how big a crew you can afford to have.

It's also almost inevitable that the larger your crew, the slower your shooting days can get.

CAMERA DEPARTMENT

- o Camera assistants
- o Key Grip
- o Grip assistants
- o Continuity

LIGHTING DEPARTMENT

- o Gaffer
- o Lighting Assistants

SOUND DEPARTMENT

- o Sound Mixer
- o Sound Assistants

ART DEPARTMENT

- o Production Designer
- o Art Director
- o Art Department Assistants

ASSISTANT DIRECTORS

- o 1st AD
- o 2nd AD

o   On set Runners

PRODUCTION DEPARTMENT

o   Line Producer

o   Production Manager

o   Production Assistants

Makeup Department

o   Make Up Artists

o   Special Effects Makeup Artists

o   Makeup assistants

Additional Departments

o   Stunts

o   Special Effects

o   Transportation

Chapter 24

IT'S ALWAYS BEEN YOU

Two promises I want you to make yourself and me after reading this book.

I want to congratulate you on completing an incredible task!

Firstly, I want you to understand that by being yourself, you possess an exclusivity that no other person has! There is only one of you and that is your superpower!

To optimize that power, I need you to start incorporating the word "yet" in your sentences. This word will tremendously impact your mindset and work flow in a positive way. For example, if you say "I don't know how to make movies", "I don't have a team", "we don't have a location", "I'll never be able to do a hundred push-ups". You may be absolutely correct and it will forever remain that way! Not because you don't have the means to train yourself to do so, but it's because you have pre-programmed and informed your brain that it is "impossible", therefore, any possible chance of converting that impossibility to a possibility will be countered by your brain. If you insert the word 'yet' to any of these sentences, for example, "I don't have a team, yet", "I can't do a hundred push-ups, yet", "we don't have a location, yet" You will relay the message to your brain that with the right steps, preparation and time, you will be able to accomplish such feats.

Secondly, look for the opportunity in every situation. During a time like the COVID19 pandemic, we were all hit in different ways. Yet, with struggle comes adapting and opportunity, especially if you're a content creator reading this book. There's more time and eyes on content than ever. Perhaps, if things were 'normal', some of this content would never be viewed or appreciated. Perhaps, you would still be waiting for your next casting audition as a performer. This is a time where new talent, fresh ideas, and great content are very much sought after since there is a void in content and limitations on big productions. This book has discussed many instances where limitations, what seemed impossible and the word 'no' presented opportunities that helped us grow our resourcefulness. Obstacles will teach you to work around them—whether you go above, below, around or over them. It will get you to think fast, and create solutions to the problems with what you've got.

FINAL WORDS

Besides choosing a very hard industry, where your work is openly displayed for criticism and you face the highest rejection in any profession, you will need to make a final choice between one of two paths as a creator in front or behind the camera.

Transactional creator, short-term. Make the movie. Create a team. Follow objectives. Get the distribution. Make the money. Try to get rich. Find another opportunity. You may reconsider a change of careers if there was no compensation involved.

Passion (Relational) creator, long-term. Make the movie because you love the art of creating or performing. You love the creative journey with its ups and downs. The relationship with the team and the vision that comes to life. You would continue to do this even if there is no payment involved.

Either one is completely up to your discretion, as long as those decisions keep you heading in the direction in which you want to go.

> ***"We don't make movies to make money, we make money to make more movies."***

> \- Walt Disney

WHAT I DID:

I used to sit at home and wait for the phone to ring for my next gig. I knew I really wanted to call the film industry my "career". I wanted to be able to make money to sustain my life and support a family in the future. It was hard, and each booking, every gig was a job. It was a contract that you knew would come to an end. You could work non-stop for a few months, then have no gigs for a year. So, I had to sit back and think. Was any of this worth it? Should I just pursue another career? Do what many people have advised me? Find a *real* job and have this as my "hobby"? Right there and then, it struck loud and clear. I knew that if there was no money involved, I would still love to create. It would be a bonus to get paid now, but again, who was I to demand pay as a starter?

I humbled myself, put my hustling mindset on and got ready to create my own work to show the world. I could have called 100 agencies that day about how much talent I thought I had, but they needed video proof!

So there you have it. As a Filmmaker or Performer. Talk is Talk. What's on paper is on paper and even though may get you a step closer, ultimately, what you need will be video of your work on FILM.

Get ready for the marathon of your life!

CONCLUSION

During the writing of this book, I would sit on the floor and meditate for a few minutes to decompress, then I would walk around under the light of the moonlight that silhouetted tree branches. I would think of revolutionary movies, motivational quotes and inspirational people.

My phone lit up through the fabric of my pocket and when I checked it, there was a message from someone that had worked with me on a few of my films. The message read, "I am just writing to tell you *thank you*! And ask if you have a gun?" The following message came in saying, "I am filming an action movie and I want you to know that I would have never thought it would be possible if it weren't for you inspiring me. Thank you. Thank you. Oh and would you like to be in my movie?"

As I responded to his text, "I'd be happy to be in your film", I smiled as it made me think of the first time I held a camera as a child. The first creative writing assignment. The first time being an extra on a film set. Then, the first film in a string of no-budget-films, that thanks to everyone that supported my visions, allowed me to have a "a ping on the radar" in the filmmakers world.

I thought about it, and wondered—what were some of the things I would've wished somebody told me when I made my first film? What guidance or little tricks could I share with people that much like me could be working on their first step on the path of filmmaking?

This simple pocketbook is the story of a man with no experience, who picked up a camera, wrote a script and didn't let his lack of film schooling impede him; a story of determination, of how I couldn't stand to see my film student friends with incredible talents get told "it was impossible to make a movie with no budget". How were they supposed to pay their cast, feed people, find locations, get the gear, finish post production? It all made sense. Money is convenient. Money buys you permits, food and gear. But, with limitation, comes innovation.

This is my pocket guide book of how I did it. The times when I fell and the times when I managed to get back up. When many friends and family members suggested if it was as easy as just that, everyone would have done it! Now, I want you to do it too.

"Good or bad, I can always just sit back and say I created something and people had a great time on set, an interesting story from being on set and good footage out of it. I also made sure I saw it from beginning to end. Now, I know what to look out for next time. It only gets easier from here."

Don't be afraid to stumble. You are not alone, and you are better than you think. Get after it!

Weaknesses that became Strengths

Valuable Lessons

The Dark Side (2009) is the first official film project I embarked on which started off as a short film then grew into a feature, the result was 17 months of non-consecutive filming. The Dark Side had 120 people onboard as cast and crew members and due to their work schedules, film shoots were challenging. Continuity over that span of time was also challenging because the seasons changed and so did the overall look and feel of some scenes. Another factor was some child actors were growing up quickly and some other actors were relocating for work, which was an inconvenience.

Lesson: If you could do it all in one go without so much time in between—do it.

After watching some of the first edits that included outdoor shots, after realizing how poor the sound was in the scenes, we needed a few more months to schedule 90% of the actors to do ADR.

Lesson: Sound is extremely important. Have a sound specialist to save you and the team extra work.

On one of the earlier shoot days we had 4 out of 10 actors call in sick. We modified the wide angles with some close ups and medium shots along with repositioning talent to make the space look less empty with the missing actors.

Lesson: Make things work regardless, for the sake of those that showed up. Cameras will let you see whatever you want it to see.

We had a cafe that agreed for us to shoot on one of the first weeks of shooting our film. Upon arrival, we saw that most of the windows were boarded and there was a sign that said they were no longer in business. With all the crew and cast there wondering what to do, we managed to ask around the area, then finally managed to get into a university cafeteria nearby for a few hours to get our scene shot.

Lesson: Think fast, stay calm and always have an alternate plan.

In one of our locations, we modified a room five times throughout different stages of the movie to serve as different locations when filming. A holding cell, a morgue, a room in a house, an office and a storage room.

Lesson: Resourcefulness goes a long way, and creativity knows no limit.

When one of the locations we had arranged to film in flooded with three-hour notice before call time, we had no option but to cancel and find a replacement. With some efficient communication with the team and a few venue owners, we secured a replacement location for free for our film a few days later.

Lesson: Sometimes things work out for the better.

When we got extra ambitious and reached out to a friend, who had a connection with chartered flights, we were able to get an aerial shot from the helicopter filming down, and from us on the ground level filming the helicopter as an insert for a later scene.

Lesson: If you don't ask, the answer is always, "*NO*".

After I nose dove into *The Dark Side* - A true story about corruption in the martial arts world and the trailer with credits were listed on IMDb, many people reached out and wanted to collaborate. A clothing sponsor, location sponsor, and picture cars sponsor wanted to get involved. By the time we wrapped, it looked like a fully-fledged production.

Lesson: Making any type of short film after a feature will be a breeze.

The Briefcase (2011)

When filming THE BRIEFCASE, we filmed a car chase scene with eight cars. An entire plan was set, describing which cars would be involved in the action, which would be safety cars and which would be camera cars. The cars were assessed for speed, smoothness (manual transmission or auto) and drivers were all tested for precision driving. The entire scene was all pre-planned on paper, then with toy cars and finally rehearsed multiple times on the road before filming.

Lesson: Rehearsal is key with people and vehicles.

One of the actors sold his car after wrapping the film. When a re-shoot was necessary, we had a different car and modified our shots from seeing the exterior of the car to shooting from the interior of the car looking out.

Lesson: More solutions, less problems.

While filming on a pier, there was one day where a gigantic ship docked next to where we filmed the first half of the scene, so we had to reposition all the camera angles and actors to work around it.

Lesson: Master the angles and cheating locations.

One of our scenes which scheduled for a 45-minute time slot, resulted in 2 hours 30minutes, due to a snow storm that started suddenly. Not only did we have to wait for the storm to end, but we also had to figure a way to melt all the snow on the ground before we started filming. With lots of walking on the snow to flatten it and using our cars exhaust to speed the melting process for some of the more dense spots, it worked like a charm.

Lesson: The only time being the Grinch is okay.

This film helped us gain the "voice trailer guy's" interest to do the voice for our official trailer back in 2011 for free when his fee typically ranges $1500 per line. The trailer received 134,000 views on YouTube.

Lesson: Work ethic supersedes talent when talent doesn't work.

The film was nominated for ten awards and won six of those awards internationally. The film also screened in two locations where all the proceeds of the film were donated to *Sick Kids Foundation* in Toronto.

After two years of doing the film festival circuits, and several years researching companies that may accept short films for distribution, we landed a half year airing contract in Anaheim while self-distributing special edition DVDs locally in Toronto.

Lesson: Promotion of your work starts when you have an idea, hire a cast, wrap the film and post it online.

VISA (2012)

On a Canadian National long weekend, a group of friends came out to help me with a comical credit card commercial idea I thought of during the week. We were able to use the patio of a friend's restaurant for free before busy hours. Borrow another friend's car to be in the shoot as long as he was on camera. The whole shoot lasted a few hours on one day.

Lesson: Short films could be used to pitch ideas for commercials. Not just cinemas.

The result was a short 30-second spot and long version 60-second spot that were both submitted to the marketing department of VISA. They loved the idea, responded back and the idea was sold to them to recreate.

Lesson: If it was just in writing, they wouldn't have seen it.

Dead End (2014)

This film was a favorite as the lead was a female, despite skepticism from industry folks. In 2015 while on set a producer and I had discussed recent work. Dead End came up and he asked to see what it looked like since it had *no-budget.* He admired the efforts and immediately thought of the next steps, to make it a feature and then a spin-off Television show. He mentioned he'd be interested to produce it for $20 million and his other producing partner may match that number if we have the right names attached to it. The talks of turning it into a high-budget-production didn't end there. He called an A-lister on the spot and she was very interested to play the part, but her agent declined due to her attachment with a superhero franchise.

Lesson: Think big, Aim small like a bullseye.

We were faced with many weather complications while shooting this as many scenes were exterior shots.

Lesson: If the seasons are on the verge of changing, get all the outdoor scenes first if possible.

When filming one scene where the car explodes and launches in the air, we managed to get a car body (empty shell) and launched it using a special catapult like platform to make it look like it blew up. When it landed, we shot that on a different day. Another visit to some junkyard and auto shops helped us secure scrap parts and tires that we could create the image of the car landed from the explosion in separate chunks. We used flammable liquid and poured it on sheets of cardboard, hid it next to the actual scrap parts, including the hole in the middle of the tire, lit it on fire and fed the fire off camera using cheap air spray deodorants to exaggerate the flames.

This film was officially announced a "milestone for women in film" and went on to win multiple awards in Los Angeles, Spain, Jakarta and Canada.

Lesson: Small efforts go a long way.

Official FIFA World Cup (2014)

I was approached by a music producer to direct a music video for the World Cup. He had researched me prior to our meeting and mentioned how he admired my hustle and work ethic that I shared on social media, hence why he approached me as the man for the job. The music video was one of the few official FIFA 2014 music videos, and only one to be shot in Toronto. With some creative visions, we were able to capture the atmosphere and vibe needed to make Toronto look like Brazil, even during the few gloomy days in September when we filmed.

Lesson: Have an open mind and innovate.

Happy to say it was a huge success when it aired and was uploaded on VEVO, YouTube and Spotify.

Lesson: Affiliations with big artists and brands will help boost your work, brand and name.

First Bust (2015)

In 2015, a Los Angeles film festival informed me I was nominated for an Icon Award. They specifically asked if I had any new action scenes to showcase for the nominees introductions.

Lesson: Always be ready to go at a drop of a hat.

I quickly wrote and choreographed a short fight scene that would take place in a bar. As people came to hear about this project and its potential award affiliation, more friends contacted me to get involved based on my previous work. Once more, people joined the team, and the length of the short fight scene expanded from an initial 2 minute fight scene to a 10 minute short film.

Lesson: Be open to help and options.

Glad to say it was a blast while filming our one day shoot with the exception of a mini tornado cutting some scenes short. We had to modify a few shots and hide in our vehicles during the tornado touchdown. It was successfully completed by the end of the day, and a year later piqued the interest of ten celebrities that heard we had intentions of making a feature based on the short. It is now in pre-production and slated to start filming in 2021 as a multi-million dollar co-production.

Lesson: 10 minutes, 10 celebrities. Quality, not quantity.

<u>Software and Submissions</u>

Here's a list of a one stop editing suite for your film projects that you can download. You will be able to tweak audio and color grade your projects. Free Trial and paid full versions available. (ios) are for apple only products.

VIDEO EDITING COMPUTERS

AVID

ADOBE

SONY VEGAS

RESOLVE

FINAL CUT PRO (ios)

iMovie (ios)

VIDEO EDITING PHONES

PowerDirector

Quik

Viva Video

iMovie (ios)

LumaFusion (ios)

KineMaster (ios)

SOUND EDITING

Some of the best free audio editors at a glance

AUDACITY

OCENAUDIO

AUDIOTOOL

ACOUSTICA

SOUNDTRACKS & SFX:

A list of some of the best places for free and paid audio, music and sound effects.

freesmusicarchive.org

bensound.com

freeplaymusic.com

purple-planet.com

premiumbeat.com

Film festival submission sites:

A list of some of the best sites to submit to Thousands of the world`s best film festivals

www.filmfreeway.com

www.festhome.com

www.filmfestivallife.com

www.shortfilmdepot.com

"TO BE A FILMMAKER, YOU HAVE TO LEAD. YOU HAVE TO BE PSYCHOTIC IN YOUR DESIRE TO DO SOMETHING. PEOPLE ALWAYS LIKE THE EASY ROUTE. YOU HAVE TO PUSH VERY HARD TO GET SOMETHING DIFFERENT."

- Danny Boyle